*Sociological Aspects of*
*Crime and Delinquency*

# STUDENTS LIBRARY OF SOCIOLOGY

GENERAL EDITOR: ROY EMERSON

Professor of Sociology
University of East Anglia

# Sociological Aspects of Crime and Delinquency

*by Michael Phillipson*

*Goldsmiths' College, University of London*

LONDON
ROUTLEDGE & KEGAN PAUL

First published 1971
by Routledge and Kegan Paul Ltd
Broadway House,
68-74 Carter Lane,
London, EC4V 5EL
Printed in Great Britain by
Northumberland Press Limited
Gateshead 8
© Michael Phillipson 1971

ISBN 0 7100 7082 9 (c)
ISBN 0 7100 7083 7 (p)

# Contents

*We beg delinquents for our life.*
*Behind each bush perhaps a knife;*
*each landscaped crag, each flowering shrub*
*hides a policeman with a club.*

Robert Lowell, 'Central Park',
(*Near the Ocean*, Faber, 1967)

*General editor's introduction*

Today sociology is going through a phase of great expansion. Not only is there a widespread general interest in the subject but there is a rapid growth in the numbers of new courses at Universities, Training Colleges and elsewhere. As a result there is an increasing number of potential readers of introductory textbooks. Some will be motivated by general interest; some will want to find out enough about the subject to see whether they would like to pursue a formal course in it; and others will already be following courses into which an element of sociology has been fused. One approach to these readers is by means of the comprehensive introductory volume giving a general coverage of the field of sociology; another is by means of a series of monographs each providing an introduction to a selected topic. Both these approaches have their advantages and disadvantages. The *Library of Sociology* adopts the second approach. It covers a more extensive range of topics than could be dealt with in a single volume, while at the same time each volume provides a thorough introductory treatment of a single topic. The reader who has little or no knowledge in the field will find within any particular book a foundation upon which to build and to extend by means of the suggestions for further reading.

The views of the man in the street on crime and delinquency are apt to show two main characteristics: first, there is an element of value judgment leading usually to the condemnation of the criminal behaviour in question; second, the explanation of the criminal behaviour tends to be seen in psychological terms. In the present book the author provides a corrective to both these tendencies. He shows that criminal behaviour is only part of a much wider class of behaviours which may be generally characterized under the heading of 'deviance'. This in turn suggests further complicated problems. Clearly, some kinds of deviant behaviour are not very seriously regarded and may simply be classed as 'eccentric'; other kinds of behaviour may be regarded with varying degrees of disapproval; but it is only a relatively small, though probably growing, sub-group of behaviours which are subject to moral and legal sanctions of a strict kind. Now, in regard to the relatively innocent kinds of deviance, we are quite prepared to admit that what is deviant or eccentric for one group is not for another. Can we argue the same way for the more serious forms of deviance? Just as we ask 'eccentric for whom?' so we must ask 'who decides that the behaviour in question is criminal?' Much recent work in criminology is based upon the possibility that some criminal behaviour may occur simply because, in the groups which manifested it, it is not regarded as criminal.

As regards the psychological explanation of deviant behaviour, no one would suggest that such an exercise is irrelevant. But it is nevertheless important to emphasize that to a great extent the explanation of deviance is to be found in sociological as well as psychological fields. This in itself raises many fascinating problems, not least in the field of philosophy, but at this point the reader may be directed to what Mr Phillipson has to say in his pages. The reader will not find any simple or glib answers to the many difficult questions which arise, but it is likely that he will emerge from his reading of this book with a much more developed understanding of what the field is and of what some of the answers might be.

A. R. EMERSON

# 1

# Introduction: some problems of traditional criminology

The sociological study of crime and delinquency raises issues which are of general importance to the discipline of sociology. These issues concern the kinds of questions which sociologists ask, the kinds of methods of investigation they use and the kinds of explanations or interpretations which they offer. One issue in particular is well illustrated by the sociological analysis of crime, and it is an issue which underlies the main arguments of this book. The fact that crime is viewed as an important social problem by some members of society raises the complex issue of the nature of the relationship between sociological 'knowledge' and problems and those things defined as social problems by the members of society in their everyday practical thinking. Can a distinction be made between sociological problems and social problems? If so, what is the relationship between the two? An underlying theme of this book is that such a distinction can and should be made and that making it has direct implications for the questions sociologists ask about the phenomenon of crime. The discussion rests, to a great extent, on the contrast which is drawn between traditional criminology and the contemporary sociological study of crime and delinquency. This comparison illustrates both the peculiar difficulties involved in the social scientific analysis of crime and also some of the ways in which the social sciences have tried to justify their claims to scientific status.

Criminology is an unusual discipline. It is the only human science which expressly takes as its subject matter a social and political problem. All the other disciplines take behaviour in general as their subject matter and select out a given level for intensive investigation. Criminology does not focus on one level of behaviour but nevertheless attempts to provide explanations of particular forms of behaviour, namely, criminal actions; as its subject matter is limited to highly particular forms of socially defined behaviour (crime), its theories and its methods are forced into the position of having to apply every level of analysis (chemical, physiological, psychological and sociological) to the phenomena which it is trying to understand. There are many problems which stem from this approach and which make the validity of criminological explanations difficult to accept. Because criminologists are often aware of the difficulties of validating their claims to provide explanations, they have to develop a rationale and justification for their activities; such a rationale has to be more than simply the interest in the drama of crime which they share with many other members of society. The criminological rationale is provided by the fact that crime in industrial societies is defined as a serious social and political problem, and the hope is that analysis of this social problem by criminologists could lead to more effective ways of dealing with it. However, the way that this rationale has been interpreted in traditional criminology raises crucial questions about its pretensions to certain kinds of objectivity and about its viability as an independent discipline. In this chapter, the

2

most fundamental of the analytical problems which face criminology are discussed briefly as a prolegomenon to the presentation of an alternative sociological perspective for the analysis of crime.

From a sociological perspective the short history of criminology has been a history of failure, and it is a failure to which sociologists themselves have made a considerable contribution. An understanding of this failure requires a critique of the kinds of questions asked by criminologists, the ways in which they try to answer them and the assumptions upon which criminology rests. Criminology, like other scientific disciplines, makes claims to objectivity, and yet it differs in one crucial respect from the other sciences: it is probably the only discipline whose subject matter is defined not by its own intrinsic qualities but by society at large and by those groups with authority in particular.

The scientist, whether natural or social, normally has the freedom to create and define his own terms, such definitions in themselves limiting his field of study. His definitions may undergo constant change in a rapidly developing science, but the changes arise out of the scientist's theories and research and not by external fiat; certainly particular interest groups in society, such as industrial or governmental, do attempt to control the direction of scientific research, but they cannot define its limiting concepts. Thus, while the area of the scientist's research can always be viewed as the product of the interplay of a range of values (stemming from the scientist himself, the scientific community, industry and government), during the course of his research the scientist's questions arise from the interests of his particular discipline and the nature of the phenomena with which it is concerned. His choice of certain styles of theories, concepts and methods, which actually define the

3

limits of his studies, arises out of the concerns of the discipline and the criteria used within it to evaluate his work.

The basic difference between criminology and other scientific disciplines is that the criminologist has his subject matter defined for him by non-criminologists; other people place the limits on his discipline. Very simply, criminology is the study of crime and the criminal; however, the sorts of behaviour defined as crime and those individuals convicted as criminal emerge out of social processes quite independent of the activities of professional criminologists. Criminal behaviour is defined by the criminal law, and law is created through a range of elaborate social processes within the political and legal institutions of industrial societies. Similarly, it is through such institutions that we set up, maintain and sometimes change the penal institutions which deal with the people who are convicted of breaking the criminal law. The criminologist thus has his subject matter given him by the society through its formal definitions of illegal behaviours – crime – and its identification of some of the people who commit criminal acts – the convicted criminals.

A recognition that the creation of the criminal law in contemporary industrial societies is a process of political conflict and compromise and that the penal system is only able to select out a proportion of all those who break the law, reveals three facts which have important implications for the explicit goals of criminology. Firstly, it is immediately clear that the legal definition of what is criminal behaviour changes over time within any society (for example, the recent changes in this country in the law relating to homosexual behaviour); secondly, different societies have different definitions of what is criminal behaviour (for example, many forms of gambling and drug use which are quite legal in this country are criminal offences in the

4

United States); thirdly, societies' reactions to crime, expressed in their penal apparatus and the institutions which 'back-up' the law, change according to time and place (for example, the abolition of the death penalty or changes in the ways in which prisons are used). This temporal and cultural relativity in relation to the social definitions of and the responses to crime mean that there is no one behavioural entity which we can call crime; there is no behaviour which is always and everywhere criminal. This crucial fact lies at the basis of the present criticism of criminology and is central to the subsequent discussion of sociological perspectives on crime and delinquency. Crime and the criminal result from social definitions and social processes. The study of crime and the criminal therefore makes criminology a 'normative' discipline, that is, one which rests initially on the evaluation by non-criminologists of what 'the problem' is; its subject matter is defined by particular social values.

Criminologists prefer to reject the suggestion that their discipline is normative (see, for example, Mannheim, 1965, I, p. 13) by asserting that the objective study of norms is not in itself normative. However, it seems possible to demonstrate criminology's normative character by showing how far its acceptance of the legal and social definitions of crime and the criminal limits its objectivity and precludes its achievement of its stated goals of explanation.

If the criminologist has his subject matter defined for him through social processes unrelated to scientific analysis, how does this impinge on the questions which he asks and the answers which he obtains? The central concern of criminology has been and still is (Mannheim, 1965; Walker, 1967; S. and E. Glueck, 1964) to locate 'the causes of crime'. This stated aim is very often accompanied by explicit and implicit suggestions that once we have located

5

these 'causes' we can do something about 'the problem' in the form of 'treatment' or 'prevention' (Mannheim, 1965, I, p. 20; Walker, 1967, p. 17). Thus, complementary to the search for 'causes' in criminology has been an interest in the reform, rehabilitation, change and control of the criminal. For example, criminologists have been very much concerned with the problem of evaluating the different penal sentences; evaluation here refers to attempts to measure the success of penal sentences in reducing levels of recidivism or re-offending among convicted offenders (Glaser, 1964; Mannheim and Wilkins, 1955). The two major areas of theory and research in criminology, then, are crime causation and the 'treatment' of offenders, the aims being to find 'the causes' and to improve 'treatment'.

Seen from a sociological perspective these aims and concerns of criminology are inappropriate because they are based both upon false assumptions about the nature of crime and the criminal and also upon implicit, and sometimes explicit, prescriptions about what society *should* do in relation to crime and delinquency; such value prescriptions are in themselves an immediate denial of criminologists' claims to scientific impartiality and objectivity. A brief examination of these assumptions may help to clarify the sociological case against traditional criminology and also suggest more appropriate perspectives for an analysis of crime and delinquency.

The key defining feature of criminology is that the criminal law is accepted as a given and becomes, therefore, the defining and limiting criterion of the discipline. In practice this has meant that criminologists have entirely ignored the study of the social processes by which the criminal law is made and changed, of the values on which it rests and their distribution in society, of the processes by which law is maintained and enforced and of the complex relationship between societal reactions to crime in the shape of the penal system and the quantity and quality of crime in a society. Refusal to ask such questions about the criminal law and the values and processes on which it is based means that criminology rests upon an implicit acceptance of the legal 'status quo'; this is, in itself, a value position and a surrender of the criminologists' claim to objectivity. This unquestioning acceptance of the values upheld by the criminal law seriously limits the type of questions which criminologists ask and also the answers which they obtain to questions concerning, for example, 'the causes of crime'. In practice this has resulted in criminologists restricting their focus in the search for 'causes' almost entirely to individuals officially convicted of criminal offences. Perhaps this limited vision and the unwillingness to question the legal processes is unsurprising in view of the fact that criminologists have traditionally been drawn largely from two of the most conservative professional groups, the law and medicine, many of whose interests the law seems designed to protect. It is difficult for such groups to undertake disinterested research into some of the very values on which their social status rests. The basic premise of traditional criminology seems to have been, therefore, that it is possible to locate 'the causes of crime' by a study of the convicted criminal population.

The protagonists of this approach attempt to locate these 'causes' through the application, in principle, of natural scientific models of explanation and methods of measurement. The debate between proponents of the natural scientific approach (positivism or determinism) and the 'free will' approach (voluntarism or intentionalism) continues in sociology and concerns disagreements as to the most appropriate perspective and methods for the analysis of social life; in criminology, however, the argument seems to have been decided, with very little debate, firmly in favour of positivism. In simple terms the criminological positivist argues that there are underlying causes for every criminal act and that his job is to define, find and measure them; he believes that there is an underlying pattern of events or factors historically antecedent to the criminal act which is its cause. This pattern of events is what the natural scientist calls the necessary and sufficient conditions for the occurrence of any given phenomenon. The criminologist is thus trying to find the laws according to which this pattern of conditions necessary and sufficient for criminal behaviour operates. In fact most of those criminologists who have applied this approach to criminal behaviour seem to have assumed that the acts of the convicted criminals could be explained by focusing on the convicted criminals alone and without reference to the encompassing social structure. The assumption is that 'the causes' can be found by an examination of convicted criminals' personal biographies and that the necessary and sufficient conditions for the commission of and conviction for a criminal act are located within these personal biographies.

If criminality is explained in terms of the biographies of individuals, a further assumption must be that convicted criminals are different in some ways not only from the few non-rule breakers in society but also from non-convicted criminals; this assumption is logically necessary, for if the constellation of biographical factors claimed to be causal can be found in some members of a non-criminal control group, they are obviously not sufficient and necessary for criminality. Assumptions about the differences between criminals and non-criminals have resulted in the predominance of certain kinds of methods in criminology; in particular, there has been much use of the comparison of samples of convicted delinquents or criminals with control

8

groups of non-delinquents matched on a limited range of variables (S. and E. Glueck, 1950). The attempt is then made through various methods to find factors which are present in the delinquent sample but absent in the officially non-delinquent control group; the differentiating factors, if found, are said to be 'the causal factors' in delinquency. No study to date has located a constellation of biographical factors which significantly distinguish convicted criminals from carefully matched non-criminals. In fact, the history of such investigations has been the successive abandonment of hypotheses which proposed that particular kinds of factors were effective discriminators (Vold, 1958); these hypotheses included the ideas that criminals were biologically inferior, mentally retarded, mentally ill, maternally deprived, economically deprived or a combination of all these plus others.

Implicit and occasionally explicit in the writings of criminologists who follow this tradition and methodology is the idea that if only such differences could be located, namely, 'the causes' of crime, then society could do something about the treatment or reformation of individual criminals; similarly, if we knew 'the causes', then we could begin to develop techniques for the prevention and elimination of crime. The kind of preventive actions or treatment programmes that would be developed would presumably be dependent on the sorts of factors said to differentiate criminals from non-criminals, but they would have one thing in common : they would all be particularistic in their restriction to a few factors. They would develop programmes aimed at 'correcting' the particular factors thought to generate delinquency or crime; if individual maladjustment were proposed as 'the cause' of delinquency, then individual counselling and psychotherapy would be the corollary treatment; if the poor physical and social

9

amenities of the community were seen as the delinquency generating forces then community projects aimed at the improvement of selected facilities would be seen as the answer; if the adolescent peer group were seen as the source of delinquency then perhaps new ways of working with youths would be proposed as ways of lowering delinquency rates. When such preventive and reformative programmes have been put into practice and carefully evaluated they have had no significant effects on community delinquency rates (McCord, 1959; Kobrin, 1959; and Miller, 1962).

The selectivity of treatment or preventive actions is the natural corollary of the highly selective and particularistic explanations of crime causation that have characterized criminology, and the failure of such remedial actions becomes understandable when viewed from the sociological perspective adopted here. Before outlining this alternative perspective, a brief review of the main stumbling blocks in the path of traditional criminological explanations is necessary.

The assumption that criminals are different from non-criminals fails to deal with the following problems. In the first place, by limiting its attention to the individuals found guilty by the courts, criminology becomes the study of the failed offender, that is, the offender who was unlucky enough to be caught and convicted. In fact, and even more narrowly, because of easy access for research, criminologists have largely concentrated on the failed offenders who have been placed in institutions. There are two basic problems of sampling here: firstly, is the convicted criminal population representative of all those committing criminal acts in a society; and secondly, is a sample of individuals drawn from selected penal institutions representative of all convicted criminals or even of all institutionalized criminals? As the answers to both these questions are in the negative, it follows that the assertions or generalizations about causation proposed by those who ignore these questions are automatically invalidated. Such questions have either been completely ignored in criminology or they have received lip service only to be ignored in actual research practice.

A second issue related to the problem of sampling concerns those offenders who, although they are discovered by either the law enforcers or others such as employers, are dealt with informally, thereby escaping public identification and the official criminal label. Restriction of sampling and research to the officially convicted criminal thus falls a long way short of the statistically acceptable sampling criteria to which criminologists nominally subscribe.

A third barrier in the way of traditional approaches to explanation is encountered in their inability to deal with those forms of behaviour which are very similar to officially defined crime in terms of motives and consequences, but which are almost completely immune from the official detection, trial and labelling processes. Many occupations, for example, provide opportunities for a wide variety of property offences (Martin, 1962); employees often claim that systematic distortion of expense accounts or the removal of the organization's stationery for personal use are simply 'perks' that go with the job (Chapman, 1968). However, their occupational immunity means that only the smallest fraction of such offenders ever receive the official criminal label.

Finally, it is worth re-emphasizing that a recognition of the cultural and temporal relativity of the definition of crime and the reactions to crime calls into question the entire approach of traditional criminology and its assumptions and thus requires an abandonment of the search for universal causes of criminality. By creating new laws outlawing different forms of behaviour (for example, in relation to the use of motor vehicles in the twentieth century) and by removing or altering old laws (for example, in relation to abortion) society is constantly redefining what is criminal and at the same time actually *creating* and *eliminating* crime by definition; these continuous processes of re-definition require different approaches to the problems of explanation from those adopted by traditional criminology.

The result of ignoring considerations such as these has meant that criminology has been an adaptive or 'norma-tive' discipline. To the extent that it accepts existing official definitions and practices as its defining criteria, it becomes little more than a covert tool of social policy and a conserva-tive force in society. The situation is one in which con-temporary criminologists make claims to the objectivity of an empirical science and then abrogate this claim by their willingness to undertake research into such social problems as the change of offenders, the evaluation of treatment methods or the development of typologies of treatment. Immediately criminologists undertake work of this kind, they move from the role of the impartial scientist and take up that of the political man; for example, in undertaking an investigation into the relative efficacy of imprisonment and probation for certain types of offenders, the criminologist, by his very willingness to carry out the project, is implicitly accepting that prison or probation are in themselves useful or appropriate for certain individuals convicted by the courts. Any research into the problems of changing offenders or preventing crime requires an implicit accept-ance of both changing the individual as a value in itself and also the value of changing him or her in the particular direction required by the society at that point in time. Such an acceptance is a political act, for it rests on both an agreement with the desirability of changing individuals and a satisfaction with the penal processes which sift out those who eventually receive the official stamp of criminality. In effect this kind of researcher says: 'those individuals sifted out by the penal system as criminals should be changed in some way, for their own good or for the good of society, and I can help to find the most effective form of change'. Acceptance of the need for change, the direction of change and the criteria for evaluating effectiveness of the processes of change all rest on values which are ultimately political in character; they are political because they reflect beliefs about how the society ought to be run and about the kinds of people society ought to contain. It must be pointed out that this is not to denigrate this sort of research in itself but rather to demonstrate its spurious claims to certain kinds of objectivity and impartiality; insofar as the criminologist undertaking this kind of research recognizes its implicit prescriptive character and hence his own part in the creation of social and penal policy, the criticism is redundant. In fact the extent of a society's willingness to undertake this kind of evaluative research may be taken as an index of its acceptance of the value of a limited rationality in social policy. Such an acceptance marks a radical break with traditional approaches to innovation in social policy in which we have acted first and thought afterwards; these issues are discussed in more detail in the last chapter.

A final problem which must be raised concerns the concept of legal responsibility. The legal systems of industrial societies are based on the concept of individual responsibility; after a series of complex legal procedures, accused individuals are found to be either guilty or not guilty of acts legally defined as criminal. Embodied in the concept of the 'guilty mind' are the ideas that the individual knew that

13

what he was doing (or not doing) was against the law and that he acted with intent. He chose to behave in a certain way knowing it to be wrong. The law itself allows that responsibility can be lessened by a range of mitigating circumstances (for example, when the victim is found to have severely provoked the attacker); this may result either in the individual being found guilty of a lesser crime, as when the person charged with murder, is found guilty of manslaughter or, at the court's discretion, in his simply being given a less severe sentence. There are, of course, a very small number of 'absolute liability' offences in which the concept of the 'guilty mind' is redundant.

The proportion of convicted persons who are found to be mentally abnormal in some way and not therefore responsible in the conventional legal sense is miniscule. Walker (1965, p. 282) shows that in 1961 they formed 0.65 per cent of all adults found guilty by the courts in England and Wales; there is a range of special court orders used for dealing with such cases. Clearly, then, over 99 per cent of convicted adult offenders were found to be legally responsible for their illegal acts. Once the court has established guilt 'beyond all reasonable doubt', it then goes on to punish the convicted offenders, choosing from the range of sentences available to it.

The penal processes involved in deciding on criminal responsibility and attached punishments enshrine beliefs about human behaviour which are rarely articulated in our everyday transactions with others; however, such beliefs seem to be so fundamental in our society as to be implicit in much of our social behaviour. These beliefs which are 'taken-for-granted' in most situations (Schuetz, 1967) concern particularly the individual's ability to choose from among a variety of projects of action; thus, in the penal system, in holding an individual to be responsible for the

14

commission of an illegal act we are saying that he could have chosen otherwise, he could have chosen not to commit the act. The public and ritual nature of legal dramas in our society effectively institutionalizes and constantly reinforces social beliefs about free will and choice. By upholding this belief in the crucial area of illegal behaviour we are granted automatic licence to extend it to the rest of our social behaviour. Thus, for most people their common-sense understanding of their world includes implicit beliefs about choice and responsibility : a man 'chooses' a wife, an adolescent 'chooses' when to pack up one job and take another or a housewife 'chooses' one brand of soap in preference to another. Our common-sense understanding of the world tells us that choice operates at all levels from our most far-reaching to our most trivial decisions.

Unfortunately, this common-sense view of social action is in fundamental contradiction to much research done in criminology and sociology, and a major problem facing sociological explanation is how to reconcile the common-sense view of the world held by the subjects of sociological investigation with the determinism of much of their theorizing and research methods. A prime characteristic of most criminological theory and research has been its acceptance of natural scientific assumptions about causation; as pointed out earlier, the core assumption seems to be that a given criminal act is simply a product of antecedent conditions – the act is determined by the preceding underlying biographical conditions of the criminal. According to this perspective the criminologist's problem is to locate the pattern of background factors which determined the commission of the criminal act; such factors could be chemical, physical, psychological or social in character. But this notion of partial determinism conflicts with the concept of legal responsibility and choice; the dilemma is this : if any individual's criminal act is determined by antecedent conditions, then how can the individual criminal be held responsible? Taken to its logical conclusion, the determinist position is a denial of the relevance of the legal and punishment process; it states that the individual had no choice but to commit the act in question. This is naïve or partial determinism because it omits to apply the same logic to the activities of the police, the judge, the lawyers and the criminological investigator himself; the complete determinist would argue that everybody's acts were determined – the judge's and the criminologist's as much as the criminal's. In this view society becomes rather like the first rehearsal of a play in which the stage is set, the parts are cast and the actors stumble more or less haltingly through their predetermined lines. Proponents of this perspective in the human sciences argue that the determinants of behaviour exist, that they can be located by getting as close as possible to the implementation of natural scientific methods of investigation and that the aim therefore of such a criminology is the prediction of criminality. By extension the proponents argue that once we have managed to predict the 'who', the 'when' and the 'where' of criminality, then we will be able to do something about it.

The persistence of the criminological determinists' basic belief that crime in general can be explained by the analysis of convicted offenders' biographies is not as surprising as may initially appear. While the other social sciences have had since their inception ongoing and heated philosophical debates about the appropriate theoretical perspectives and methodological styles to adopt in their analyses of the social world, there has been a complete dearth of this kind of discussion within criminology. The continuous questioning of its philosophical basis and the assumptions on which it rests, which has characterized sociology, is completely absent from criminology, and one can look in vain through the academic criminological journals for any fundamental debate about the assumptions on which it rests. This absence of internal philosophical debate within criminology has contributed considerably to the persistence of naïve assumptions about causation and prevention; the absence of self-questioning also reinforces the view that criminology, in claiming scientific status, is laying a thin veneer of academic respectability over its implicit ideology.

The way that the positivist perspective has been applied in criminology and the results of its application suggest that it is based on mistaken and limiting assumptions about social behaviour in general and criminal behaviour in particular. The alternative perspective adopted here is based on different assumptions, has different aims, has different methods and has a different subject matter to those of traditional criminology. The approach is, on the one hand, more encompassing in that it moves away from the narrow focus on the individual convicted criminals to the broader issues of situations, social processes and social structures and, on the other hand, less imperialistic in its rejection of the search for universal causes of crime with its implicit prescriptions for treatment and prevention. The broad outlines of this alternative are presented in the next chapter.

# 2

# An alternative perspective

If a sociological perspective is to improve on traditional criminological orientations, it must come to terms with the stumbling blocks which impeded the development of criminology; whilst it is recognized that such a perspective will inevitably face different analytical problems of its own, the suggestion here is that these problems do not have the inherently intractable character of those faced by traditional criminology. The core problems to be overcome are those of the scope and level of analysis, the related problem of the normative character of criminology and the issue of individual responsibility. No attempt is made here to provide an all-embracing theory of crime and delinquency; rather, a perspective is presented which orients the observer or investigator to certain kinds of analytical problems and questions and, at the same time, by-passes the criminological stumbling blocks. Some general features of this perspective are outlined before its solutions for the traditional problems are spelled out.

The proposed perspective places the study of crime and delinquency within the broader and more inclusive sociological analysis of social deviance. Following Cohen (1966), social deviance can be defined simply as behaviour that violates normative rules; normative rules refer to those guides for behaviour which orient an individual's actions in any interaction with others. These normative rules and expectations can range from the 'taken-for-granted' implicit guides which go unquestioned by the actor in his everyday activities, such as the rule that directs men in our society to wear trousers, through the more formal rules for action which operate in work, educational and other formal organizations, to the most explicit and formal set of rules embodied in the criminal and other kinds of law. It can be seen that in sociology the concept of rule has a wider meaning than in our everyday use of the word; in everyday usage we tend to think of a rule as an explicit formal statement which tells us what we should or should not do in given situations. The rules of organized games epitomize our everyday usage of the term: the 'rules of the game' are agreed in principle by all the participants before the game commences, and the mutual agreements to abide by them furnish the conditions which allow the game to begin and proceed. Similarly, at school or at work there are usually formal, precise statements which attempt to furnish the conditions for orderly interaction by stating the boundaries of acceptable conduct. However, the sociologist extends the everyday meaning of the term 'rule' to include those guides for behaviour which may be relatively informal, implicit and frequently unstated in the course of our interaction with each other. By including in the term 'rule' the complete range of guides for behaviour, from the most formal to the most informal, from those operative in an individual's most trivial to those in his most important decisions, the sociologist is making his task very complex; whilst it may seem an apparently simple task to define the most formal rules and their conditions of applicability, at the other end of the continuum the definition of the implicit and informal rules may be an extremely complicated exercise.

Thus one of the basic assumptions which informs socio-logical investigation is that there are rules or norms which serve as guides for the action of the participant in all situations of social interaction; it follows that a prime task of sociology is to analyse the content and the various qualities of these rules or norms. In particular, the sociologist would want to describe the conditions of applicability of any given rule, especially the range and types of situations in which it was applicable and the range of social statuses and roles which were subject to it. The flexibility of the rule would be important too, that is, how far individuals were free to modify it or to implement their own verbal or behavioural interpretation of it. A thorough analysis would also require a study of the history of the rule : how did it emerge, who created it and whose interests did it represent initially? Does it still represent the same interests or have these changed? A necessary corollary of these questions about the derivation and qualities of the rule would be the study of reactions to deviations from it; this would entail asking a range of questions about how the rule is maintained or enforced. The kinds of sanctions used to deal with those who deviate from the rule, from physical violence to mild social disapproval, and their effects would similarly be a central concern of this approach.

These considerations mean, in effect, that the study of social deviance becomes, as Cohen points out, the study of deviance, conformity and control. Deviance can only be understood effectively within this more inclusive perspective which relates questions about why people deviate to questions about why people conform, with particular emphasis being placed on the contribution of techniques of social control to the deviance-producing processes. This perspective proposes that the amount and quality of deviance in a society or any part of a society is the product of the interaction between deviants and potential deviants, and the society's or group's social control mechanisms. It is therefore necessary to look at both sides of the coin to understand deviance, that is, both at those who deviate and in what situations and also at those who attempt to enforce the rule and with what techniques and effects.

Implicit in this approach is the view that an understanding of conformity, that is, of the 'normal' or the 'non-deviant', is an essential complement to an understanding of the 'abnormal' or deviant. The question is asked: 'Can we really understand the abnormal unless we thoroughly understand the normal first?' Posing this question draws attention to a further failing of traditional criminology; all too frequently criminologists and sociologists made assumptions about what they considered to be the 'normal' or the 'non-criminal' and prejudged the abnormality of the criminal. The assumption was made that 'normal' people did not break the law and that therefore those who did must be 'abnormal'; their law-breaking was viewed as a symptom of some inner abnormality or pathology.

The investigators' assumptions about what was normal rested typically on their own personal, usually middle-class, values; behaviours which deviated radically from the investigators' strongly held but implicit personal values were diagnosed as abnormal, and the roots of the abnormalities were sought either in physical or psychological pathologies. A failure to spell out the dimensions of normality and their distribution in society meant that assertions about the abnormality of offenders by criminologists rested on their common-sense assumptions about the rightness and wrongness of some behaviours. Diagnosis of abnormality thus frequently coincided conveniently with strongly held moral beliefs, so that behaviours felt to be morally wrong from one ethical standpoint were consequently also diagnosed as pathological. This resulted in much tautologous argument in which the convicted criminal was defined as 'abnormal' or 'pathological' because of his criminality, and then this assumed 'abnormality' was used to explain his criminality. So unless the investigator carefully defines what he means by 'normal' and actually shows how it is distributed within society or a social group, then many of his assertions about the 'abnormal' or the 'deviant' may be based on entirely false assumptions about the normal dimensions of the behaviours which he is investigating. An essential prerequisite of any analysis of deviance in relation to a given rule or norm would seem to be the clear and precise definitions of the non-deviant together with some attempt to show its empirical distribution in society, rather than the traditional reliance on assumptions about the distribution of normality.

According to this perspective, then, criminal and delinquent behaviours become particular examples of the general phenomenon of social deviance. The processes involved in deviation from specifically legal norms can be compared to the processes resulting in other forms of deviance; the sociologist argues that analysis of the similarities and differences in the processes of deviance from substantively different norms should enhance sociological understanding more than the study of any given form of deviance in isolation. This perspective opens up an enormous range of subject matter for the student of social deviance; not only does it include many of the behaviours traditionally designated as social problems by society, such as crime, mental illness, narcotic addiction and alcoholism, it also includes areas not so designated. For example, certain kinds of unconventional or innovative behaviours can be viewed from a social deviance perspective. Thus, social groups which are concerned with modifying or breaking accepted canons of practice in any sphere, from the artistic to the political, can be seen as deviant; many occupational groups in our society are granted licence to deviate from accepted styles and practices in their occupation: artists of all kinds, fashion designers and certain kinds of scientists all have licence to innovate stylistically and change accepted practices.

Very often this licence to innovate stylistically, which is granted both by other artists, their typical 'reference group', and also by large sections of the public, is accompanied by a more general expectation that artists will also be unconventional in their behaviour; when they meet these expectations their flouting of conventions is generally tolerated. The social tolerance accorded to artists' stylistic and behavioural deviations contrasts with the lack of tolerance shown to other deviant groups.

In the fields of religious or political behaviour there are groups whose ideologies, beliefs and behaviours are sufficiently different from the conventional political and religious approaches of a society to render them deviant. Moreover, this kind of deviance may not be as remote from criminal deviance as it might initially appear; it may be that different forms of deviance emerge in the same parts of society and that any individual might as easily become a political or religious deviant as a criminal or narcotic addict. This kind of consideration might be relevant in any analysis of deviance in some of the black ghettoes of the large American cities where a range of extreme political and religious sects flourish alongside narcotic and criminal sub-groups. Taken to its logical conclusion, this approach proposes that deviance can be studied in any situation where social norms exist as guides for action; wherever there is a social group, deviation from its norms can be studied, whether the norms are formal and precise or implicit and ambiguous. However, as will be suggested sub-

23

sequently, a more circumscribed and limited use of the concept of deviance may help to increase its clarity.

Apart from the difficulties peculiar to this perspective, can such an approach come to terms with the problems faced by traditional criminology? Let us take the scope and level of analysis first. The limitation of criminology to a focus on the convicted criminal meant that its explanations of crime and criminality rested on hypotheses and research relating to the convicted criminal population alone. Further, in terms of aim, the kinds of explanation proposed, whilst claiming to explain crime and criminality in general, in practice offered explanations of individual criminality, that is, what caused any given individual to commit criminal acts. The social deviance perspective on crime differs radically both in focus and in aim; convicted criminals become only one particular group of legal norm breakers whose processing by the penal system may have important implications for their subsequent criminality. The main focus would be on the processes of creating, maintaining, enforcing and breaking of legal and allied norms, these processes in their turn only being understandable by their placement in a societal context. The aim would not be the explanation of individual criminality in terms of a group of individual biographical factors, but rather an understanding of the social nature of crime as the constantly changing product of a wide variety of complex social processes. An integral part of this aim would be the demonstration that the quantity and quality of crime in a given society is inseparable from the prevailing conditions of life at the time of analysis. In other words, crime can only be understood by showing how intimately it is bound up with the non-criminal features of a society. To take crime out of its social context and to try to explain it as the product of a minority of unfortunate individuals apparently 'outside' the bounds of

24

conventional society has been a cardinal sin of traditional criminology.

The deviance perspective also comes to terms much more satisfactorily with the value problems involved in the scientific analysis of crime than does traditional criminology which, as we saw in chapter 1, is a normative discipline. An unquestioned acceptance of the legal status quo, with the related refusal to ask certain kinds of questions and the willingness of criminologists to involve themselves practically in evaluating or recommending reformative, preventive, treatment and punitive penal programmes epitomize the normative character of criminology; they are the 'value' problems which contradict criminologists' claims to objectivity. The deviance perspective has as its fundamental aim the improvement of sociological understanding and not 'the solution' to the social problem of crime and delinquency. The key distinction in approach would be that the investigation of norms and deviance from them would be empirical, that is, it would attempt to describe and interpret the actual norms which acted as guides for action; it would be the actors' typical definitions of the situation which would define the normality or the deviance of their activities and not the investigators' assumptions about what was normal. What the sociologist tries to describe and understand are the many characteristics of the norms which actually orient people's conduct in their interaction with others; this necessitates focusing on the meanings which individuals give to the multitude of situations faced in everyday life and describing the patterns which these social meanings form. By describing these patterns of social meanings which guide behaviour, and which are created, maintained and modified by the actors themselves, the sociologist can prevent the intrusion of his own assumptions and values to a much greater extent than was possible within the limited and

25

normative focus of traditional criminology.

In this perspective, legal norms are simply seen as one group of norms among many; they are abstract and formal and may enter any individual's consciousness only rarely as actual guides for action; the social deviance approach proposes that the sociological understanding of the distribution of the violations of legal norms in society and the complementary distribution of reactions to such violations can only be derived from a knowledge of the actual norms which orient people's behaviour. Fortunately, this daunting task is partially simplified by the remarkable consistency which characterizes patterns of social interaction. An illustration of the implications of such an approach can be given by the following example. The traditional assumption that property offences are almost entirely confined to the lower working class is quickly called into question when middle-class behaviour is actually examined; thus many property offences are viewed simply as occupational 'perks', and this is reinforced by their immunity from law enforcement. In this case functionally equivalent behaviour – removing property that does not belong to you – is given different social meanings both by those undertaking the behaviour and those responsible for enforcement (Chapman, 1968). A major sociological task is to analyse the norms which actually orient actions in everyday situations and to examine the social processes through which these different social meanings emerge and are maintained.

In the non-normative approach, then, the sociologist takes the actor's own definitions and meanings as his data and does not allow his own value assumptions about, for example, the necessity for law and order, to guide or limit his data selection. This is a simplified description of the non-normative approach, and it raises many theoretical and methodological issues that are central to sociology in general; some of these will be elaborated in subsequent discussion.

The final problem with which an alternative perspective has to come to terms is the issue of individual responsibility. The dilemma to be faced is the irreconcilability of the legal and everyday common-sense models of behaviour on the one hand with the deterministic scientific models employed in traditional criminological analysis on the other. Models of the former generally see the individual as possessing, within certain limits, choice or free will, whilst deterministic scientific models propose that the phenomenon to be explained (such as a criminal act) is 'caused' or 'determined' by antecedent conditions. Thus the ultimate implication of the deterministic model is to deny the legitimacy and relevance of legal and common-sense models of man. If everything is determined, the idea of choice becomes superfluous. It was suggested in the first chapter that traditional criminology was particularly characterized by deterministic theories and methods; its styles of theorizing and investigation rested on the same sorts of assumptions as those upon which the natural sciences rest in their explanation of natural phenomena.

In fact much sociology has also been and still is characterized by these deterministic approaches to explanation, and the debate continues about the most appropriate perspective for the sociologist to adopt towards his subject matter (Winter, 1966). Briefly, the debate is between two broad groups. There are those who claim that social phenomena and natural phenomena are very similar, that therefore the application of scientific methods and assumptions to social phenomena is appropriate and that eventually sociologists will be able to formulate laws about social behaviour in the same way as natural scientists derive laws. The other side is represented by those who argue that social phenomena are fundamentally different from natural phenomena and that therefore the kinds of statements which can be made about social phenomena will be unlike the laws of natural science. This assertion of the fundamental difference between social and natural phenomena stems from the fact that the objects of the natural world, have no inherent meaning, whereas social phenomena only exist through their meanings. Similarly, protagonists of this viewpoint would suggest that natural scientific methods and assumptions have only a limited usefulness in sociology because they can only tell part of the story and other methods are needed to complement them. A central difference of the two approaches is found in the stance of the observer towards the social phenomena being studied. The theories and methods of the deterministic criminologist view man as an object whose actions are determined by internal and external forces, whereas the sociologist in the tradition of subjective interpretation (which was first formulated coherently by Max Weber) sees man as a subject possessing choice (Weber, 1949); the subjective sociologist's methodological problem is to describe and understand (Weber's notion of *verstehen*) the typical patterns of choice. The term 'subjectivity' refers both to the investigator's method of arriving at an interpretation of social phenomena and also to the kinds of data to which he gives primacy, namely, the subjective meanings of the actors whose activities he is trying to understand.

One distinction between the two approaches which is very relevant to the analysis of crime concerns their goals : one goal of natural scientific investigation is to locate *the* cause or the *causes* of phenomena, while the goal of the other perspective is not 'the causes' but rather certain kinds of 'understanding' or interpretation of social phenomena. This understanding is qualitatively rather different from

28

causal explanation; essentially it seeks to understand the processes by which actors arrive at their particular pattern of choices and to describe the actors' perceptions of the limits of these choices. The methodological procedures through which such an understanding can be obtained are rather different from the classical scientific method; these differences should emerge more clearly in the subsequent discussion of actual research projects and theories concerned with crime and delinquency. For the sake of brevity the two approaches will be referred to as the objective (natural scientific) and subjective (non-deterministic, interpretive) approaches to explanation; traditional criminology epitomizes the objective approach while the proposed alternative perspective adopts the subjective model.

A basic implication of adopting the subjective approach is the abandonment of the search for the universal cause or causes of crime and a recognition that crime can only be understood through a knowledge of the particular social structure and social processes within and through which it occurs. The cultural and temporal relativity of such understanding contradicts the search for universal causes.

In the light of these two approaches how can the issue of individual responsibility be dealt with? The suggestion here is that the most effective explanation is one that comes to terms with common-sense understandings and beliefs about choice and especially with the fact that most people in most situations see themselves as possessing a range of choices of action. Because the implicit assumptions of the objective approach, by denying that the actor can choose between projects of action, are out of line with legal and common-sense understandings of action, this suggests that the subjective approach is more appropriate for the understanding of social phenomena. Unfortunately, space precludes more than a passing mention of this debate between the subjective and objective approaches which lies at the centre of the sociological rationale.

Two further justifications are proposed in support of the subjective approach. Firstly, by adopting the subjective approach, attention is drawn to something which has been largely ignored by criminology but which is given a certain importance in our legal processing of criminals and which is accorded importance in everyday explanations of criminal or any other behaviour. This is the actor's motivation. From a subjective perspective motivation is a central focus of analysis, for the sociologist argues that motives are socially learned and are differentially distributed in the social structure (Gerth and Mills, 1961); his interest centres on the shared patterns of motivation, their meanings for a social group and the ways that these are expressed in action. Much importance is thus given to the social meanings which actors give to their own and others' behaviour and to the situations which they experience. An individual's explanations of his past activities and of his future intentions constitute for him the 'why' of his behaviour or his motivations, and it is these which become some of the most important raw data for the subjective sociologist. However, the sociologist's main concern is with the *social* character of motivation rather than with each individual's unique pattern of motives; his interest is in the shared motives, in the socially typical rather than the uniquely personal. Thus an analysis of the social distribution of patterns of motivation, how motives emerge, are learned and transmitted, becomes central in this perspective; the sociologist tries to understand men's actions by examining the social bases of their motivation.

This differs from traditional criminology in a fundamental way. Motivation was rarely seen as important in itself in explaining crime and delinquency; it was simply a by-product of preceding forces. According to the objective perspective, these preceding forces determined motivation so that a study of actors' motivations was superfluous; what was important was to locate these preceding, underlying forces. Values, attitudes and beliefs, of central importance to the subjective sociologist and closely bound up with patterns of motivation, were largely disregarded by criminologists in explanations of criminality. On the rare occasions when they were considered, for example in psychoanalytic explanations (Friedlander, 1947; Glover, 1960), they were viewed largely as a means of getting at the 'real' underlying explanatory factors in the criminal's life experience and as expressions of the actor's unconscious wishes. In other words, the actor's stated values and motivations were hardly ever taken at their face value as meaningful and important data in themselves. It ought to be added that the subjective sociologist does not go to the other extreme and accept uncritically everything that his subject tells him as being a reliable account of events or his own beliefs; the problem of ascertaining the reliability and validity of any individual's statements lies at the heart of methodology in sociology, and the confidence which the sociologist can place in such statements will depend particularly on the kind of relationship which he had with the respondent, the sort of situation in which he obtained the information and the nature of the information sought. Nevertheless, if these problems can be overcome, the subjective sociologist views an individual's stated beliefs as valuable data in themselves which contribute directly to the sociologist's understanding and interpretation of patterns of choice.

The fact that this emphasis on patterns of stated values and motivations is in line with our everyday commonsense and our legal explanations of conduct is directly related to the second justification for the subjective perspective. If the sociologist uses the same sort of data in his explanations and interpretations of events as other members of the society use in their interpretations, this ought to facilitate his task of making his explanations meaningful to the members of that society. The social scientist's problem of communicating his explanations and interpretations of events and processes is important for practical reasons. Firstly, the sociologist is frequently employed directly by somebody seeking answers to or data about what, for him, is a problem; thus, after completing his research, the sociologist has the task of making his findings meaningful to his sponsor. Secondly, at a more abstract level, the entire relevance of sociology to its social context can be called into question if its models of explanation cannot be translated into terms which make sense to the vast majority of non-sociologists in the society; if it is difficult or impossible to translate sociological interpretations into terms which make sense to members of the surrounding society, this would seem to call into question the viability of the discipline. For example, it could be suggested that extreme forms of behaviouristic psychology, in which extrapolations are made from animal behaviour and applied to human behaviour, have already reached the situation of alienation from everyday explanations of conduct in society.

Thus the kinds of models of man with which sociology operates appear to be very relevant to the meaning which people give to sociology in a society. If it operates with models of man which are very different from the common-sense models by which people operate, it will be seen as largely irrelevant, and the problems of communication between sociologists and non-sociologists will be acute; on the other hand, the closer the congruence of sociological and everyday common-sense models, the easier are the problems of communication and the more relevant are the sociological interpretations to the members of the society. The explanation or understanding of crime and delinquency provides a very good example of this problem, for it is in this very field that our society continually upholds and reinforces common-sense beliefs about choice and individual responsibility; thus for the sociologist or criminologist to offer explanations of crime which are based on opposing deterministic models of man would be to directly contradict a very basic common-sense assumption which underpins our social structure.

The subjective approach therefore directs the sociologist's attention to what people actually think and feel about their own and others' actions and is based upon assumptions about man which are relatively in tune with the common-sense assumptions of the members of the society. What kind of interpretations are offered which purport to take account of our assumptions about individual responsibility and choice?

It was suggested that the subjective approach does not look for *the* cause or the *causes* of crime but offers certain kinds of understanding and interpretations of crime and delinquency by placing them in the wider context of social deviance. The subjective sociologist would argue that there is a range of levels of understanding and that the most satisfactory solution to the problem of explanation occurs when an interpretation considers each level and shows the logical continuity of understanding between each level; an adequate understanding would rest on the provision of data at each level and an interpretation which made sense of these data by showing the links between levels. Many of the sociologists who have proposed theories of crime or delinquency have passed over or have made assumptions

33

about one or another level of understanding. They have concentrated on the study of one level in both their theorizing and their collection of data, at the same time making explicit or implicit assumptions about the other levels which would fit in with their interpretation and their data. What are these levels of understanding which need to be integrated for a satisfactory understanding? Such analytical divisons tend to be arbitrary, but as an illustration three levels are distinguished here to demonstrate the explanatory problems involved.

The first level at which it is possible to make statements about crime and delinquency is that of the total society being studied, say, the United States or England and Wales. This is the most abstract level of understanding because the kinds of statements made at this level are the most remote from the concrete activities of any individual or group; broad generalizations can be made about apparent trends in crime, but the kind of generalization or interpretation proposed will tend to depend on the particular theoretical stance taken by the observer and hence upon the assumptions which he makes about the other levels of understanding. Not only do we have the law (which is said to apply to all members of society equally) as a 'given' at the level of the total society, but industrial societies also publish a mass of official statistics relating to crime, the activities of the police and the courts, and the penal system; at the same time the official book-keepers are producing a mass of other official statistics relating to almost every aspect of our lives from income and expenditure to mortality patterns. Given this welter of data it becomes possible to correlate one set of statistics with another, to see whether changes and trends are random or statistically inter-correlated; the compilation and correlation of a multitude of indices relating to most aspects of

34

our social life is, with the aid of the computer, a straight-forward task, and social scientists frequently use such official statistics to bulwark their interpretations of social events.

However, there are two kinds of assumptions made in using such statistics on their own in an explanation of crime or any other activity. Firstly, the assumption has to be made that the statistics are actually measuring what they claim to be measuring; in other words, can we 'trust' the official organizations and take the statistics at their face value? This question raises the sociological problem of the reliability and validity of official data. Secondly, a set of assumptions has to be made about the actors who have been so neatly summed up in the official statistics; in particular, assumptions have to be made about the kind of people they were, about the situations which they faced and about their motivations. This second type of assumption rests upon models or theories of what man is like, and, as we have seen, there is considerable disagreement among social scientists about this fundamental issue. Both sets of assumptions, then, are statements of the investigator's faith, unless they are supported by empirical data; such data can only be acquired by analysis at the other levels of understanding. Thus, interpretations which are offered at one level of analysis, whilst they may be consistent with the data available at that level, may not be congruent with data and interpretations at other levels.

For example, a problem of contemporary criminology has been to explain the continuing rise in officially reported property offences in a period of increasing affluence. Simple economic explanations, which viewed poverty as the main motivating force of such crime, have been replaced by more complex theories like that of Merton (1963), which explains such deviance as a response to the size of the

35

disparity in different parts of society between the goals people strive to achieve (particularly material success) and the actual means provided for their achievement; this will be dealt with in more detail subsequently. However, this theory at the level of the total society rests on certain assumptions about individual behaviour with which many sociologists would disagree and which certainly have not been tested adequately empirically. Thus, while Merton's theory may fit the official facts at the societal level, at the experiential level of the acting delinquent or criminal its basic assumptions may be largely unfounded.

A second level of analysis might be that of the local community or neighbourhood. Many of the prescriptions for social action in relation to delinquency, which may have arisen out of such sociological research into urban delinquency patterns as that of social ecologists like Shaw and McKay (1942) in the United States, are based on explanations of delinquency at the level of the local community. They often seem to view the community as something quite autonomous and separate from the wider society, generating delinquency through its own internal social forces. Thus, high rates of delinquency in one area can be explained in terms of the particular characteristics of that community, such as inadequate play facilities, poor housing or insufficient involvement and participation of members of the community in their own self-government. The assumption seems to be that the social processes flowing from such features are peculiar to that community and need not be related to its position in the wider social structure. Such a view of the local community may have been more appropriate to the rural communities of pre-industrial societies but is somewhat divorced from the social realities of the mass society in which the inhabitants of any sub-community have a series of complex interrelationships with the central government and other communities. The penetration of any community by other communities and by the formal institutions of the total society is a taken-for-granted part of the world of the man in mass society. Any interpretation of delinquency and crime primarily at the level of the local community should be concerned mainly with the ways in which the particular community is both typical of all such communities in that society and also an integral part of the wider social structure and only secondarily with its unique features.

Finally, explanations at the individual or face-to-face level can all too easily omit a consideration of the forms of the relationships and processes which bind an individual indissolubly to the surrounding community and to the total society. These omissions characterize much of the writing and research into crime and delinquency which might be labelled as social psychology; the main emphasis is placed on the study of the direct social pressures which an individual experiences in his face-to-face relationships with a variety of others. In the field of delinquency, for example, a study of the more important face-to-face relationships might compare the relative importance of family and peer group values and ties to the adolescent and the relationship of such values to delinquent behaviour patterns. The individual is seen as being at the intersection of a range of sometimes conflicting and sometimes congruent immediate social pressures to conform to particular values and norms. However, a sociologically meaningful interpretation of delinquency would have to relate such data to the other levels of analysis; on their own they form only a small part of the total picture. Thus, the complex relationships between the individual, the community and the total society must be described and placed within a cohesive framework if an adequate interpretation of crime and delinquency is to be offered.

From the viewpoint of the subjective sociologist the problem is one of trying to understand the patterns of choice in any given part of a society, and he views such choice-patterns as emerging from the social meanings which people give to their world. Thus, study of the processes of emergence, transmission, maintenance and modification of social meanings lies at the centre of his approach. He hypothesizes that the social structure of a society can best be understood as a vast shifting complex of social meanings. In this context social meanings refer to the shared symbols by which individuals experience, understand and describe the situations which confront them. These symbols are invariably expressed in language by the actors; it is through language that an individual expresses his future intentions, his explanations of his past behaviours and the current meanings which he gives to his experiences and his relationships. An individual makes sense of his experiences through language and communicates his experiences to others largely through the medium of language (the few exceptions being the plastic, visual and aural arts; even here frequent attempts are made to translate the 'meaning' of artistic products into linguistic terms, the typical case being that of the critic). Thus the forms which linguistic expression take in different parts of the social structure, the range, style and complexity of linguistic expression, are given considerable importance by the sociologist. As he can only understand and interpret social meanings through language, it ceases to be simply a useful medium of communication and becomes an object of study in itself. This is not to say that the sociologist reifies language in making it an 'object' of study; he does not view it as an object which has some kind of independent effect on the outcome of a course of action, but his focus on language is rather on its role as the prime carrier of cultural meanings and man's main medium of self-expression. The work of Bernstein (1960), an English socio-logist, and his analysis of the relationship between linguistic communication styles and social class position is important in this connection.

Thus social meanings, invariably expressed through lan-guage, are seen as underlying the actors' pattern of choice and hence their social action. In analysing these meanings the sociologist is concerned not with the individually unique but with the socially typical; shared and common meanings are viewed as leading to socially typical actions. The socio-logist's interest is therefore in the differential distribution of the meanings given to their experiences by social groups. It is this distribution of meanings which comprises the social structure. Within this perspective the social structure is viewed as a structure of typical social meanings. Social organization comprises typical responses to typical situa-tions; these typical responses arise out of the socially shared or inter-subjective processes of interpretation and meaning-construction. Perhaps the word 'typical' should be qualified in case it gives too static a picture of social relationships. By 'typical' is meant those aspects of atti-tudes, beliefs and actions which are shared with others; thus, in relation to any cultural item which is studied, the sociologist accepts that every individual has his own unique perspective, experiences and interpretations, but he is con-cerned with the essence of what is common to the members of any group in their interpretations.

For example, do the boys who occasionally go on shop-lifting expeditions together, in spite of the differences in their individual emotional responses of fear, detachment or excitement, share common interpretations of the events?

Do they typically give the same kind of explanation for their activities? Do their explanations vary according to whom they are explaining the events, so that their typical explanations to their mates differ from their typical explanations to their parents, which in turn differ from their typical explanations to juvenile court magistrates or inquisitive sociologists? Posing this kind of question suggests that any event can have several typical meanings and that such typical meanings will depend very much on the context and relationship in which they are given. A comprehensive understanding of the meaning of any kind of event depends on the sociologist's ability to describe these different meanings and show how they are congruent or in conflict with each other.

How then does this style of analysis cope with the problem of choice? An individual's choice in any given situation, that is, the way in which he eventually decides to act, is seen as arising out of the social meanings which he gives to his world; in their turn these meanings can only be expressed symbolically, invariably through language. Thus analysis of the differential distribution of social meanings between groups in a society provides a basis for understanding how the groups symbolize their experiences and their relationships with others. In terms of choice the sociologist wants to know the range of alternatives which were weighed up by the actor before a particular alternative was chosen; in most situations our actions arise out of a process of reflection in which we weigh up the consequences of alternative forms of action. It is the content of this process of reflection, in terms of the symbolically conceived alternatives which are weighed up against each other, that the sociologist attempts to lay bare. What emerges from this kind of analysis is that for any given typical situation there is a picture of typical courses of

40

action, placed against a backcloth of a limited number of perceived alternatives; the individual's actual choice in any situation arises from these perceived alternatives. Most importantly, in terms of the question of determinism, the subjective sociologist argues that any actual choice is indeterminate or unpredictable and arises out of the particular content of the individual's stream of consciousness at the moment he makes the choice; as this can never be known fully, so actions can never be fully predicted. So the sociologist is left with placing any given response within the context of typical responses to that kind of situation.

There are two distinct problems here. Firstly, there is the question of innovation and how new responses emerge either to the same or to new situations. In some senses the question of choice seems to be much more important here because the typical responses to new situations do not yet exist and there are usually no clear guides for action or expectations of behaviour; thus, understanding the way in which the alternatives are perceived is crucial for the analysis of innovatory acts and the emergence of fresh styles of action. Secondly, there is the maintenance of typical responses to typical situations; here responses or solutions to the typical situations have already been worked out and are frequently well established or institutionalized. They are given to the newcomer as the accepted ways of dealing with the situation. In this case the form of the perceived alternatives will be different from that of the first situation; acceptance of the existing typical responses will depend not so much on the process of weighing up and reflecting on the perceived alternatives but rather on what the individual takes-for-granted in his social world, on the things he never questions. Both these problems are relevant to particular theories of delinquency which attempt to deal with the emergence and maintenance of what various writers have referred to as the delinquent sub-culture.

The view of choice which the sociologist adopts, then, is inevitably a compromise between fully-blown determinism and a state of completely open consciousness. David Matza (1964), whose work will be considered later, refers to this compromise as 'soft' determinism. Essentially the subjective sociologist argues that certain kinds of limitations typically operate on an individual's choice, and his task is to show the limitations within which choice seems to operate fairly consistently. The limitations or restrictions on behaviour are almost always social rather than physical; only in extreme situations, such as contact with society's formal agents of social control like the police or prison officers, is the choice of adults limited by physical pressures. The source of such social pressures is always other people, yet, crucially, these pressures are not external to us in any way (except in the limiting case of physical force), for they are composed of our internal symbolic constructions of such pressures. They comprise in particular the ways in which we anticipate other people will act in response to our own intended acts or words. These pressures may seem to arise from many different sources but in fact emerge primarily from our own past experiences and our command over the linguistic symbols of the culture; the way in which we internally symbolize and anticipate such pressures calls forth our responses to them. In this process they also become inseparably bound up with our motives for any proposed course of action, so that motivation can only be understood by relating it to our conceptions of other people's expectations of our behaviour. Motives are therefore always socially grounded.

Thus the sociologist's major interest becomes one of making sense of or understanding the world retrospectively

42

by describing the typical patterns of choice which operate, and by showing the relationship between these patterns and the different levels of understanding. The importance of precisely predicting the future in analogous ways to natural scientific predictions recedes if this perspective is adopted. As Gibson Winter says:

> The social world is dynamic whereas the grasp of that world in human science is fixed. Human action looks forward in its projects; human science looks backward to grasp the meaning of human action in terms of the past. This characteristic of human science marks its limits as a predictive and controlling discipline; human science talks about the future only on the assumption of continuity of past patterns of action. On the other hand, the value of human science arises from its explication of the conditions of human projects, bringing to consciousness many aspects of the social world which lie hidden from view and identifying regularities which give relative predictability to the social world. (Winter, 1966, p. 121)

Such a perspective has many ramifications for both the conceptual and methodological problems of sociology and particularly for the kinds of statements and interpretations which the sociologist wants and feels he is able to make about social relationships. His concern is to offer certain kinds of interpretations of social processes rather than to make precise statistical predictions about the future. Abandoning the precise predictive role may also impinge directly on the social and political importance which is accorded to sociological interpretations and methods, thus changing common-sense understandings of the nature and aims of sociology.

The most important advantages of adopting this particular sociological perspective for the analysis of crime and delinquency can now be drawn together and summarized.

Firstly, the value problem of traditional criminology is overcome; the subject matter is no longer defined for the investigator by existing legal norms and the mechanisms of the penal system. His field of study is defined by the norms and values of his discipline rather than by the existing legal norms of the society. The questions which the investigator asks will only occasionally coincide with those asked by the society, and as soon as he explicitly tries to answer the society's questions the sociologist runs the risk of tying himself to the values of powerful social groups and thus becoming a political instrument of those in power rather than an analyst.

Secondly, placing the study of crime and delinquency into the mainstream of sociology widens the perspective on crime and opens up the possibility of new levels of understanding. Moreover, sociology itself stands to gain from this assertion that crime is a social process, for the aim is to improve sociological understanding and not to solve social problems.

Thirdly, and related to the last point, the sociological perspective stresses the similarity between criminal and other actions in society. Far from emphasizing the difference between criminal and non-criminal acts and thereby treating the criminal as an isolated phenomenon excluded from society, this approach draws out the similarities between crime and other social processes. By placing the study of crime in the wider context of social deviance, the analysis of the processes which generate other forms of deviance, such as mental illness, narcotic addiction or professional misconduct, may give new insights into and a better understanding of criminal behaviour. Study of the processes which are common to the generation and maintenance of different types of social deviance leads to fresh perspectives on particular forms of deviance such as crime.

44

Fourthly, the hard determinism of many previous approaches is abandoned, and the sociologist tries to come to terms more realistically with the problem of choice. This fulfils two purposes: firstly, it reasserts the importance of the philosophical underpinnings of sociology and points to the necessity of examining the basic assumptions about man on which sociology and criminology rest; secondly, it asserts the inseparability of sociological theories or perspectives from research methods and practices which are too often treated as separate, independent parts of the discipline. Inevitably the emphasis on choice goes hand-in-hand with a very conscious realization of the dynamic nature of social life and moves the sociologist towards focusing on social processes and interaction patterns rather than the presentation of a static picture of social life that characterizes not only traditional criminology but also much sociology. Crime is no longer seen as 'objectively given' but becomes, in the terms of Rubington and Weinberg (1968), 'subjectively problematic'; that is, the very processes by which certain acts are defined and labelled as criminal and the consequences of such processes are viewed as arising from the subjective meanings which actors give to their experiences and are therefore problematic both for the actors and for the investigating sociologist. They require investigation and understanding and cannot simply be accepted as objectively given. This approach is not one-sided for it emphasizes the interaction between a society's social control mechanisms and the individuals and groups who eventually become successfully labelled as deviant. It is these processes which are seen as generating the amount and quality of deviance in a society.

The fifth advantage is related to the subjectively problematic nature of the processes studied by the sociologist and relates to the use of official statistics on crime and the

45

penal system. Industrial societies annually produce a mass of criminal statistics which are used by the press, by politicians, by the public and all too frequently by criminologists and sociologists to draw general conclusions about the changing patterns of crime in a society and, by extension, about the society's changing 'moral climate'. Such data, when viewed from the alternative perspective, become problematic in themselves and cannot be accepted as 'givens'; far from assuming that they necessarily reflect 'real' trends in the amount and form of crime in a society, they are seen rather as arising out of the very complex processes of interaction between offenders, victims, members of the public and formal agencies of social control. As noted previously, it is these very processes which the sociologist views as problematic and requiring investigation. He is inclined to see these official statistics much more as indices of the activities of the official organizations than as reflecting the 'real' patterns of crime in society (Cicourel and Kitsuse, 1963a). Official agencies sift out and record only a tiny fraction of all the illegal behaviours in a society, and their sifting and selecting processes should be problematic for the sociologist.

Finally, if the implications of this perspective for social policy in relation to crime and delinquency are considered, they may suggest why the programmes of prevention, punishment or treatment which have been directed without exception at the individual offender have signally failed in their aims of change. The sociological perspective suggests that major changes in social structure would be required to effect changes in the patterns of crime and delinquency in a society. Even assuming that such structural changes were to occur, crime would not disappear but would rather change its character. The impossibility of eliminating crime is a taken-for-granted canon of the sociological perspective, and this normality of crime will be discussed in the next chapter. In relation to the kinds of social changes which might be required to alter the character and amount of crime in a society, it must be emphasized that such changes are of a political nature, and it is not part of the sociologist's task to make recommendations about social change, for the form of such recommendations will depend on the individual sociologist's personal values. The sociologist can only pose the questions and the dilemmas for society and not the answers, for the latter will only emerge through political action and processes. These issues will be taken up in more detail in chapter 6.

If these are the main advantages and justifications for such a perspective, something must be said briefly about the other side of the coin, about its difficulties and disadvantages.

At the most general level, the major difficulty seems to be that of the almost unlimited scope of the perspective; placing crime and delinquency in the much more inclusive study of social deviance creates inter-related difficulties for theories and research. If deviance occurs in every social situation where there are norms of behaviour, it seems likely that the generalizations about deviance which could be derived at this overall level would contribute very little to our understanding of any particular situation simply because they would be so general. Cohen's definition, therefore, of deviance as norm-violating behaviour is too general and requires modification. Some limitations on the scope of the deviance perspective or some breakdown of the field into substantive areas of study according to the similarities in the deviance-generating processes is called for. For example, while on the one hand it might be difficult to draw parallels in the processes involved in cheating at cards and large-scale company frauds, both clear forms of deviance, on the other hand the similarities in our labelling, processing and institutionalization of mentally ill persons and criminals and delinquents are much more obvious. It seems necessary therefore to develop criteria for meaningfully subdividing the vast amorphous area of social deviance; such criteria might be defined by questions concerning how generally the norms which are being violated are held, whether the norms are supposed to apply to everybody in a society and are formally enforceable like the criminal law or whether they apply to only small select groups and are informally enforceable, and whether the identified deviant may be taken out of circulation or whether he is always allowed to remain within the community. If the analogies between deviance in different kinds of situations are to be meaningful rather than empty and naïve, then the main parameters of deviance must be defined and the field of study subdivided accordingly.

One such approach which attempts to limit the use of the term social deviance and to give it more clarity is offered by Lofland (1969). Taking the nation-state or total society as his reference point, he sees deviance as one kind of social conflict. He differentiates types of conflict according to criteria relating to the character and relations of parties in conflict and distinguishes deviance from simple non-conformity, civil uprising or disorder, social movements, civil war and mainstream party politics. He thus narrows the definition of deviance down in these terms:

> Deviance is the name of the conflict game in which individuals or loosely organised small groups with little power are strongly feared by a well-organised, sizable minority or majority who have a large amount of power....
>
> A primary indicator of 'this type of conflict called deviance' in a total society is, then, the existence of

48

state rulings and corresponding enforcement mechanisms that provide for the possibility of forceably removing actors from civil society, either by banishment,
annihilation or incarceration.... Deviance is rule violation only in the limited sense that it involves violating
the rules of relatively large minorities or majorities who
are powerful, well-organised and highly fearful of individuals or loosely organised or small groups who lack
power. (Lofland, 1969, pp. 14, 18, 19)

Lofland's approach overcomes the difficulties of Cohen's
all-inclusive definition of deviance. Yet his category of
deviance is still sufficiently broad to provide a basis for
comparing apparently very different forms of deviance,
like crime, mental illness, narcotic addiction or even physical disability.

A further difficulty with the deviance perspective arises
from defining what is 'normal'; as suggested earlier the
study of deviance requires a concomitant concern with conformity, for, before one can effectively define and describe
what is deviant, one must have clear definitions of the
norms from which deviance occurs. It is easy enough to
assume, for example, in the case of crime and delinquency,
that the normal is defined by the criminal law, but in practice this assumption may be entirely misplaced; normal
behaviour can only be defined as that which actually occurs
and is seen as acceptable under the circumstances by the
actors. The abstract principles embodied in the criminal law
tell us little about the actual values which guide behaviour
in concrete everyday situations. While in traditional criminology assumptions were made about the 'norm', in the
social deviance perspective defining the normal goes hand-
in-hand with defining the abnormal or the deviant; both
are subjectively problematic. It may be just as difficult in
many situations to define what is normal as it is to define

what is deviant. This may be particularly the case with criminal behaviour, which of necessity involves acts in which the actors generally try to keep their identities a secret; even when non-participants are 'in the know', elaborate methods may be utilized to preserve their silence. Perhaps in these circumstances it is not so surprising that the criminologist abandoned the study of actual norms and behaviours and restricted himself to studying the failed offender. The most difficult problem faced by the investigator of deviance is to define and describe the actual normal values and behaviour of any individual or social group as opposed to the 'respectable' values which offenders lay over their 'unrespectable' activities.

This leads directly to the third and conceivably the most crucial problem facing the deviance perspective – that of the development of methodological styles appropriate to the assumptions and concepts of this approach. If for the purposes of understanding and interpretation, the perspective lays greatest emphasis on the social meanings which actors give to their situations and on the processes of social interaction, that is, on the dynamic character of social life, then the methodological problem is one of using techniques which lay bare social meanings and describe interaction processes in the most reliable way possible. In this context the idea of reliability relates to the investigator's ability to provide interpretations which, on the one hand, make sense at the common-sense level of understanding (that is, which are understood by and acceptable to the actors themselves) and, on the other hand, are integrated with data and concepts at the other levels of meaning and understanding discussed earlier. The social meanings and interaction processes may not be easily elicited or observed in many areas of deviance. Restriction to the established and most common techniques of sociological research may give only a very

60

limited and partial understanding of the processes of deviance, for they may be unable to strip off the mask of respectability with which much deviance may be covered.

A further limitation to the traditional sociological techniques of investigation is that they present relatively static pictures of social life, whereas the deviance perspective requires a focus on processes and social dynamics. Typically the sociologist's research techniques centre around the use of various kinds of interview techniques involving the use of questionnaires and schedules and the analysis of organizationally produced records and data; less frequently used are content analyses of written documents such as letters, newspapers, magazines or books. It happens that the least frequently used styles of research, namely, certain kinds of observational techniques in which the investigator typically lives in the milieu of the group which he is investigating, are those which seem most likely to provide the sociologist with reliable data on the social meanings which actors give to their situations.

These styles of participant and non-participant observation, in which the sociologist literally tries to place himself in the situations of his subjects and to see the world through their eyes, may be particularly relevant to the study of deviance in which the investigator's problem is to understand those very processes and meanings which the deviant invariably attempts to conceal from prying eyes. The social distance which usually exists between deviant and researcher may be reduced through the deviant's acceptance of the investigator in his milieu; however, it may take considerable time for sufficient trust to build up to effect this reduction. Unfortunately, this style of research is undertaken only occasionally in sociology, and there are very few studies in the field of deviance which typify this approach (the work of W. F. Whyte, 1966, Liebow, 1967 and Polsky,

1967, are valuable exceptions in the study of deviance and related fields). When it has been done it has invariably laid bare levels of meaning which would have been unobtainable through the conventional sociological research techniques; at the same time such descriptions have a vividness which contrasts favourably with much arid sociological research reportage.

From the point of view of the standard canons of sociological methodology, which models itself on a stereotype of natural scientific method, this kind of research has many problems of its own. Insofar as sociology is seen as a science which tries to offer explanation in terms of cause and effect models of behaviour, the observational techniques are viewed as having a rather limited value. A methodology based on natural scientific models of investigation sees observational styles of research as too dependent on the abilities and personality of the individual researcher and therefore as very difficult to replicate. The question asked is: would any other researcher undertaking observation of the same group or community have found the same things? Clearly, as data resulting from such techniques arise from the interaction between the researcher and his subjects, such research is highly personalized; however, insofar as this kind of researcher is concerned, like any other sociologist, with the typical rather than the unique, and providing he is honest enough to record his own feelings and responses as well as those of his subjects, it is suggested that these techniques must be integrated more effectively into sociology and must be seen not merely as subsidiary techniques but as essential and viable methodological styles (Bruyn, 1966).

Thus the main methodological problems for the deviance perspective are, firstly, to develop research techniques which describe levels of meaning essential for the understanding of deviance and which are largely unreach-able through conventional techniques and, secondly, to inte-grate these techniques with their own assumptions and problems into the mainstream of sociology.

To conclude this introduction to the deviance perspec-tive, the major questions with which such an approach would have to deal are briefly outlined, as these form the basis for some of the subsequent discussion.

Firstly, at the most basic level, the sociologist must answer the question : is crime or, more generally, deviance in some form inevitable, that is, is it an inherent feature of social organization? Certainly, all the empirical evi-dence points to the universality of crime, but does this necessarily mean that crime is logically bound up with the conditions necessary for society to exist? This issue of the normality of crime is a fundamental one for sociologists, for the way in which it is answered has implications both for the kind of explanations of crime which can be pro-posed and also for utopian beliefs about the possibility of eliminating crime.

More specifically, the second kind of question asks how we can understand the particular patterns of crime which characterize any given society. There are two distinct steps to be followed in answering this question. A description of the character of the society's crime must precede any attempted interpretation, and such a description may not be easy, for the deviance student closely questions the reliability of the picture of crime presented in the official criminal and penal statistics. Only if this problem of des-cription can be adequately overcome can the question then be asked: why this pattern as opposed to any other? Answers to this question would always rest on certain philo-sophical, sociological and psychological assumptions about the nature of man and about the nature of the phenomena

53

which sociologists study, but essentially the task of interpretation would be to show the relationships between criminal and deviant phenomena and other social processes and institutions. In effect, the sociologist argues that an understanding of crime can only come from a demonstration of how closely it is bound up with other aspects of social life. Far from treating it as a separate, autonomous entity the sociologist attempts to show how the pattern of crime is inextricably intertwined with the network of social relationships comprising the society. The distribution and pattern of crime in the society will suggest those aspects of the social structure towards which the sociologist's analysis will be primarily directed.

The third fundamental question is, in practice, closely bound up with the previous one; however, as it has received little attention in sociological interpretations of crime and delinquency until recently, it is worth emphasizing its importance separately. The question asks about the attempts to control and regulate crime in a society: what are the dominant processes of social control in relation to crime? In posing this question the sociologist would investigate the processes by which the criminal is selected, identified, labelled and punished and through which the society attempts to effect changes in criminals and to prevent crime. In fact the answers to this question would complement the answers obtained to the previous question, for the deviance theorist would argue that there is a dialectical relationship between, on the one hand, the amount and character of deviance in a society and, on the other, the attempts to prevent and control such deviance. Rates of deviance are a product of the interaction between potential and actual deviants and the agents of social control, and changes on one side of the equation will call forth changes on the other. The sociologist's problem is to describe the ever-changing relationship between the two halves of the equation.

Finally, and underpinning each of these questions which are largely concerned with general social processes and issues of social structure, the deviance perspective poses questions which are designed to clarify sociological understanding of individual projects and courses of action and to place these within their social context. An understanding of the ubiquity of deviance, the particular forms it takes in different social structures and its relationship to social control processes rests on the study of the typical structures of social meaning at the face-to-face level of analysis. The perspective sees the meaning structures of individuals as created, maintained, modified or drastically changed in ongoing processes of interaction and individual interpretation. The inherently creative individual is viewed in his socially meaningful actions as constantly involved in the creation, maintenance and validation of a self, an identity. Thus sociological analysis and understanding of deviance and control at the inter-personal level, recognizing creativity, attempts to place individual actions within the context of the socially typical. Some of the kinds of analytical issues concerning the self and face-to-face interaction, which are seen as important in the deviance perspective, such as the distinction between primary and secondary deviation, the development of deviant identities or the move into a deviant group are discussed in more detail in chapter 4. Understanding the human meaning of deviance and control at the inter-personal or intentional level arguably poses the greatest conceptual and methodological challenges to the sociologist.

# 3

# The paradox of social control and the normality of crime

This chapter discusses some aspects of the ubiquitous character of social deviance and social reactions to it. All known societies have socially defined rules, individuals who break them and ways of dealing with those rule-breakers who are caught. Two important complementary interpretations of aspects of this universality – by Durkheim and Mead – provide a key part of the conceptual base of the deviance perspective, and the analytical questions about crime and its control which are suggested by these inter-pretations are very different in character from those of traditional criminology. Each author deals with different aspects of the relationship between, firstly, the character of social organization and the definition of crime and, secondly, the individual and the society of which he is a member. Their analyses of the social sources of the rules outlawing certain behaviours as deviant provide a basis for the study of deviance within particular societies. A question that arises in Durkheim's analysis concerns the possibility of a society without crime (Durkheim, 1950); whilst ques-tions about logical possibilities are marginal to sociology, which as an empirical discipline, is concerned with what actually is rather than what is theoretically possible, the answers which Durkheim provides to this question are integral to his discussion of the normality of crime. As the idea of the normality of crime is a central tenet of the deviance perspective and at the same time a contradiction

56

of much common-sense thinking about crime, it is worth considering this question in some detail.

In trying to answer the question 'Is a society without crime possible?' we have to move away from culture-bound definitions of which actual behaviours constitute crime in any given society to a consideration of crime as an abstract category. Instead of thinking of crime, for example, in terms of those particular behaviours which are outlawed typically by the legal systems of industrial societies, we have to turn to those features of crime which are common to many different types of societies, from the institutionally complex to the apparently simpler societies. The strands binding the many different societal definitions of crime together are the common social processes involved and not the diverse contents of what is actually defined as crime; the abstract category of crime then becomes those behaviours which are outlawed by societies' laws or customs and which, if undertaken and detected, call forth certain responses from the societies' agents of social control. These controlling responses are public in character, usually of a ritual or ceremonial nature, and are carried out by agents who claim to represent the communities' dominant interests.

This tells us that there is no such thing as 'natural crime'; there are no acts which are always crimes *in themselves* irrespective of cultural definitions. Crime comprises those classes of behaviour which, if committed in certain social contexts and ways, are defined as crime by the laws or customs of the society. This approach again emphasizes the cultural and temporal relativity of the definition of crime and also lends support to the substitution of the concept of 'deviance' for that of crime; use of the deviance approach directs attention away from culture-bound definitions of crime to the general social processes involved in publicly outlawing and sanctioning deviant acts and individuals.

That no behaviour is inherently criminal can be demonstrated by showing that even those acts which our society considers to be the most heinous crimes, if they are performed in certain circumstances, not only cease to be defined as crime but may also become praiseworthy acts: killing is legitimated on a vast scale in time of war or when it is performed on our behalf by the public executioner. In both cases there are many people, such as pacifists and abolitionists, who, in terms of their personal values, would define even such officially legitimated killings as 'murder'; these grave disputes at the level of public debate concerning the meanings attached to the act of killing illustrate the importance of analysing actual social definitions of crime rather than relying on the abstract letter of the law. Similarly, in our law, for killing as for any other crime, mitigating circumstances can dramatically reduce the severity of society's reactions to functionally equivalent behaviours. What we might define as child murder was seen as perfectly legitimate by the Spartans when they tested the survival capacity of their newly born infants by placing them on the frosty roof for a night. Rape, by definition, cannot exist within marriage, although the act itself – forced intercourse – may be functionally equivalent to a comparable act which was committed outside the bounds of marriage and given the official label of rape.

Crime in any society, therefore, comprises those definitions of acts which *in certain specified situations* are outside the official rules of that society; in their turn the official rules are reflections of a range of values which are more or less strongly held within the society, either by most people for most of the time or by smaller interest groups which are sufficiently well organized politically to

58

enforce their values through the official rules and the official agencies of social control. The question of the political organization of minority interest groups is especially important in relation to law maintenance and law reform in industrial societies where many governmental decisions may be the results of conflicts of interest between competing pressure groups. In England, for example, recent changes in the law relating to abortion reflect the compromise of interests reached between such organized competing pressure groups as the Roman Catholic Church, the medical profession and the Abortion Law Reform Association. Definitions of the content of crime are undergoing constant changes and subtle modifications, and even though the laws themselves may not be changed, the meanings given to the law may shift in their emphases; such changes in meaning may be observed in the cases where laws remain on the statute book but are rarely invoked or enforced. This would suggest that the content of the official statutes at any point in time may provide only a moderate introductory guide to the patterns of values which are actually held to be publicly enforceable at that time; if we are looking for those values, they can only be reflected in the actual patterns of deviantly defined behaviours and the controlling responses which they call forth. These patterns of actual control activities are the direct reflection of those values which are important to the society or the organized segments of society, and beliefs about what is important undergo constant change.

Clearly crime, then, can only exist if there are some publicly acknowledged and enforced rules of conduct in a society. If we could find or logically conceive of a society either without rules at all or with a set of rules which *everybody kept all the time*, then the view of crime as inevitable or normal would have to be rejected. However, if

59

such a society is both non-existent and inconceivable, apart from in our fantasies, then crime must be viewed as a normal phenomenon, as something which is inevitably present wherever society is found.

Two sociologists from very different intellectual traditions offer complementary perspectives on this issue and provide the logic on which rests a taken-for-granted tenet of contemporary deviance theorists, namely, that crime must be viewed as a normal phenomenon because it is bound up with the very conditions of existence of society. Let us consider their discussions briefly.

The French sociologist Emile Durkheim was the first sociologist to deal theoretically with the question of the normality of crime. In *The Rules of Sociological Method* Durkheim (1950) argued that the sociologist could establish the normality of any social phenomenon by answering two complementary questions, the first of which was empirical and the second theoretical. The empirical question asked: is the particular social phenomenon to be found in every known society? If the answer to this was 'yes', the theoretical question was then asked: is it logically bound up with the conditions necessary for group life? For Durkheim these were the two essential criteria of normality: the first, being simply a statistical operation, would demonstrate the ubiquity of the phenomenon and the second would be the logical explanation of this ubiquity. The example which Durkheim chose to illustrate this method was that of crime.

First he pointed out in answer to the empirical question that every known society possessed both rules outlawing certain behaviours which offended 'strongly held collective sentiments' (p. 67) and also individuals who occasionally did offend such sentiments and drew 'upon themselves penal repression'. The ubiquity of crime was empirically

60

indisputable, but how was it logically inevitable and therefore necessary?

To answer this second question Durkheim focused on the relationship between the individual consciousnesses of the members of a society and the collective sentiments embodied in the criminal law. His argument makes the following points:

i. For any category of criminal behaviour to disappear completely from a society there would have to be unanimity of feeling amongst all members of the society towards the behaviour. All would have to feel sufficiently intensely about it to rule out the possibility of its committal.

ii. Given this increase in intensity sufficient to prevent the occurrence of certain acts (for whatever reasons it occurred), crime would not disappear but would simply change its form; the changes in the intensity of the unanimous collective sentiments would mean that those behaviours which were previously regarded as 'simple moral faults' (p. 68) would take on the status of crimes in the changed society. In Durkheim's own words:

> Imagine a society of saints, a perfect cloister of exemplary individuals. Crimes, properly so called, will there be unknown; but faults which appear venial to the layman will create there the same scandal that the ordinary offence does in ordinary consciousness. (pp. 68-9)

iii. The elimination of dissent (deviance or crime) from society is impossible because it would require absolute uniformity of consciousness among all the individuals in a society. Such a uniformity of consciousness is precluded by the nature of consciousness itself. It is not even possible for two individuals, let alone all the members of a society, to even approach identity of consciousness. Disagreement is built into the fact of the uniqueness of individual experience and so therefore is the inevitability of deviance.

An English sociologist, Wilkins (1964), uses the statistical normal curve distribution to illustrate his theory of deviance, and a modification of his use of the normal curve may help to illustrate the logic of Durkheim's argument. In the Figure (p. 63) the area under the normal curve represents the volume of social acts of the society; in the motto of a well-known national newspaper: 'All of life is there'. The original curve imposed on the baseline (AC) might be taken to represent activity in society as we know it, with actions ranging from the most honest act (A) to the most heinous crime (C) and with the law (B) cutting off as illegal a proportion (X) of the acts performed in the society. To eliminate crime as we know it, the baseline would have to move up to $(A_1C_1)$, following the heightened intensity of the collective sentiments; however, it is clear that there are still extreme forms of behaviour in the new society which are outlawed following the increased intensity, so the legal cut-off point moves to $B_1$ and the outlawed acts become $X_1$. Following each heightening of intensity, one batch of acts disappears altogether to be replaced by another batch which attract similar penal repression; note that the volume of acts in society is getting smaller and smaller following each heightening of the intensity of the collective sentiments. Finally, with the coincidence of $A_n$, $B_n$ and $C_n$, we arrive at the ultimate situation of no social action. In other words, the more behaviours that are eliminated through the increasing intensity of the collective sentiments, the less action there is in the society. Taken to its ultimate absurdity the argument suggests that the collective sentiments at the apex of the curve and their intensity would outlaw all action in society, at which point society would cease to exist.

It is the logic of this argument which leads Durkheim to

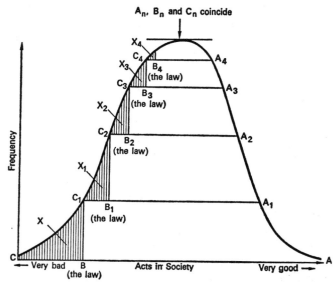

conclude that a society without some form of crime or deviance is a contradiction in terms; deviance, in other words, is bound up with the conditions necessary for society to exist and results from the unique nature of individual consciousness. Naturally this argument goes against many of our accepted beliefs and hopes about deviance and its punishment, treatment and prevention; it also serves as a salutary warning to the builders of utopias that the elimination of all forms of deviance cannot be achieved. Accepting the normality of deviance means, as Durkheim also pointed out, accepting its usefulness or rather recognizing that the collective sentiments which are sufficiently flexible to allow for criminal deviance by this very flexibility allow also for the possibility of social change through individual originality. The flexibility which allows the criminal to exist also allows the political, re-

63

ligious, artistic, scientific or immediately practical innova-
tor to co-exist alongside him. All these individuals or groups
are deviating from the culturally accepted ways of thinking
and acting and are putting forward alternatives to existing
beliefs and practices.

It must be emphasized that Durkheim was talking about
the normality of crime and criminality and not about the
normality of the individual criminal. These are two analytically distinct questions which are levelled at different
phenomena; the question of the normality of crime is
answered at the cross-cultural level of analysis and refers
to total societies, whereas the question of the normality
of the criminal can only be meaningfully posed about individual criminals *within* a given society. As mentioned
earlier, the criteria of individual normality and abnormality
are culturally specific, so that the definitions of individual
criminals as normal or abnormal can only be understood by
examining the criteria of normality in that society.

A complementary perspective is provided in an essay by
the American philosopher and social psychologist George
Herbert Mead entitled 'The Psychology of Punitive Justice'
(Mead, 1918). In this essay, while he is not explicitly concerned with normality as such, Mead perceptively discusses
the symbolic meaning of the criminal law and punitive
justice to members of a society. The characteristic societal
response to the criminal is to punish him, and Mead
attempts to account for the particular forms of social
organization which reflect society's hostility towards the
criminal and their implications. The two most frequent
justifications for punishment of the criminal are retribution
and deterrence.

Initially we justify punishment by arguing that the criminal deserves to be punished simply because he has committed the crime; by committing the crime he has given
64

members of society the right to inflict retributive punishment. The justification of deterrence is one of social expedience, and it is through this that we decide the severity and form of the punishment; the emphasis shifts from simple retribution to the idea of prevention through deterrence. We believe that we can effect some kind of commensurability between the severity of the punishment, the assumed deterrent fear which we believe it inspires in both the offender himself and future potential offenders, and the extent to which we feel aggrieved by the criminal's actions. At first sight then, Mead argues, our punishment of the criminal seems to reflect these two justifications of deterrence and retribution, and yet these two principles are insufficient to explain the socially organized reactions to the criminal. If these were the only principles involved, the kind of penal process that would emerge would be some kind of lynch or mob law which would inevitably operate in a random way. Mead finds the key to the problem of understanding our punishment of the criminal in what he calls the 'majesty of the law', in the 'assumed solemnity of criminal court procedure' and in the 'supposedly impartial and impersonal character of justice'. In other words, he focuses on the public ritual and drama of the criminal trial, which he sees as reflecting the 'theoretically impartial enforcement of the common will' and through which justice is to be done 'though the heavens fall'.

He likens criminal court procedure to a battle between the contending parties; the very nature of this battle serves to define and reinforce our emotional attitudes towards the two parties for 'the emotions called out are the emotions of battle'. In this battle the law is presented as both the defender of the community and the attacker of the enemies of the community, so that insofar as each member at all identifies with the wider community, he sees the punitive process defending him and attacking the offender on his behalf. The basis of the criminal law, as reflected in the drama of the penal process, appears to lie in its dual purpose of, firstly, arousing in law-abiding members of the community 'the inhibitions which make rebellion impossible for them' and, secondly, of stigmatizing the offender either by removing him from the community in the extreme case or by some lesser form of stigmatization arising from the ritual public labelling process. Even for minor infractions of the law the public nature of the judicial process which provides the offender with an official criminal record serves to label and stigmatize him effectively as an enemy of the community. Such stigmatization may have far-reaching implications for the offender's identity and moral career.

The conflict nature of the confrontation between the law, which protects abstract rights of the community members, and the criminal suggests that the hostile attitude reflected in retributive and deterrent punishments is inescapable. Indeed, Mead goes on to suggest that this attitude of hostility cannot be reconciled with the principles of treatment and reform of the criminal; the aims of punishment, on the one hand, and eradication of the causes of crime, on the other, seem to be mutually exclusive. In Mead's terms, 'as long as the social organization is dominated by the attitude of hostility the individuals or groups who are the objects of this organization will remain enemies. It is quite impossible psychologically to hate the sin and love the sinner' (p. 228). He thus calls into question the logic of the current attempts of the penal systems of industrial societies to combine punishment with techniques for changing criminals. There is an irreconcilable conflict between punishment and treatment.

66

The main result of this attitude of hostility towards the criminal is, Mead concludes, a sense of social solidarity : community members who otherwise have quite divergent individual interests unite in their solidarity against the common enemy; they submerge their differences and unite in their hostility towards the law-breaker. Indeed this sense of social solidarity may be the crucial way of holding the community together and of defining its limits; insofar as the convicted criminal is responsible for this social solidarity by attracting public hostility towards himself, he seems to be making a major contribution to preserving and defining the boundaries of the community. In fact Mead does not see the criminal as presenting a real threat to the permanence of the community, but he does see him as calling forth a social solidarity that continually serves to reaffirm and reinforce the community's values concerning members' rights and duties.

The idea that the criminal does not present a real threat to the structure of society perhaps requires some clarification. What Mead seems to imply is that the criminal is of necessity secretive and that the clandestine nature of his activities does not provide a basis from which to radically change the social structure; far from wishing to change social relationships through his activities, the criminal prefers to be devious within the existing social arrangements. He can never pose a real threat to the social structure because he is not offering a viable alternative; any social organization which he does undertake in the course of his activities is concerned only with the isolated criminal project in hand, and he poses no major threat to structural arrangements. In contrast the political rebel has as his central motivating force the desire to change the social structure, so that while he may, of necessity, remain secretive in the early stages of his activities, he can only achieve

67

his aims by eventually obtaining some kind of public support; he is forced at some stage to come out into the open if he is to succeed. For the criminal to step into the open and declare his intentions at any stage would be to invite disaster for his project. It seems then that the criminal prefers to work at the margins of the existing community boundaries rather than to consciously attempt to redefine those boundaries. Conventional criminal activities are committed in spite of the law and not with a view to changing it.

In fact the penal system treats many explicitly political rebels in the same way as it treats those found guilty of the more conventional criminal activities so that they may consider themselves inadvertently and wrongly labelled 'criminal'. The small minority of political criminals whose aim is to effect certain political changes by making their declarations of intent and actions public do pose a visible threat to the existing power structure, and if they step close to the margins of legitimate political protest, they immediately call onto themselves the punitive repression which is normally reserved for the secretive criminal. The main differences between the two types of criminals seem to lie therefore in their intentions and in the openness of their activities; the nature of these differences supports Mead's contention that the conventional criminal poses no real threat to the social structure.

Two major apparent exceptions to this are the cases of organized crime in the United States and the organized criminality of Hitler's Nazi regime; but in both of these cases the patterns of crime are so intimately bound up with the political structure and processes that they must be considered as special cases and not simply as examples of exaggerated conventional criminality.

By focusing on the characteristics of the hostile attitude to the criminal as reflected in the social meanings given to the criminal law and the punitive penal processes, Mead both complements and adds to Durkheim's discussion of the normality of crime. His analysis of the emergence of the processes of hostility, social solidarity, public labelling and consequent stigmatization of the criminal suggests how the interaction between the criminal and the penal system confirms a community's moral boundaries by constantly defining and reaffirming what is permissible and what is not. These definitions and reaffirmations keep alive the sense of what the community means and is.

The unavoidable dilemma of whether to punish or attempt to change the criminal is also clearly stated by Mead; reformation can only come through a positive under-standing of the criminal and not through negative punish-ment, and yet positive understanding leads to a denial of the criminal's responsibility and therefore of the relevance of his punishment. This immediately takes us back to the question of responsibility and choice; the positivist who would omit choice from his explanation of the criminal act denies the criminal's responsibility and by doing so denies the relevance of punishment. Contemporary penal systems are subject to a variety of conflicting pressures, ranging from aggressive hostility to the criminal to demands for extensive penal reform, and they still sit firmly astride the horns of the punishment versus change dilemma.

The problems or role conflicts facing social workers em-ployed in the penal service epitomize this dilemma. Proba-tion officers, for example, are firstly officers and servants of the criminal court; they are thus regarded by convicted offenders as punitive agents, and they may often be directly involved in the enforcement of the civil and criminal law. On the other hand, the ideology of social casework, in whose underlying principles probation officers are instruc-ted during training, runs directly counter to the punitive principle. It rests on the building of a trusting relationship between caseworker and 'client' with a view to helping the client to an understanding of his 'problems' which would enable him to help himself. The 'problems' diagnosed by casework ideology are typically derived from the untested and often untestable assumptions of psycho-analytic theory and may bear little relation to what the client would define as problematic. But the main point in this context is the conflict between the demands placed on the probation officer as a punitive servant of the court and the requirements of the professional social work ideology. Their irreconcilability illustrates the problems involved in trying to implement reformative or therapeutic measures based on certain kinds of understanding of 'the problem' in a punitive setting.

Apart from his discussion of the normality of crime, Durkheim also provides an analysis of punishment which closely parallels that of Mead. His work *Moral Education* (Durkheim, 1961) includes an analysis of the role of punishment in the school in which several of his insights and hypotheses concerning punishment are generalizable to official punishment for infractions of the criminal law. He argues that the essential function of punishment is not simply retributive, nor is it to produce individual atonement, nor is it to deter the offender, but rather it is to demonstrate the inviolability of the rule broken by the offender. Thus, Durkheim argues, the pain produced in the punished offender is only an incidental repercussion of punishment, and the severe punishment of an act is only justifiable to the extent that it is necessary to make public disapproval of the act 'utterly unequivocal'. Suffering is thus merely a secondary element in punishment and in some circumstances may be totally lacking, for the publicly observed punishment may not be experienced as suffering by the offender; an example of this might be probation for those offenders for whom it is a mere irritation. The crucial element in punishment, then, is the affirmation in the face of an offence of the rule that the offence denies. In Durkheim's words:

> If nothing happens to neutralize its effects a moral violation *demoralizes*. What must there be to rectify the evil thus produced? The law that has been violated must somehow bear witness that despite appearances it remains always itself, that it has lost none of its force or its authority despite the act that repudiated it. In other words, it must assert itself in the face of the violation and react in such a way as to demonstrate a strength proportionate to that of the attack against it. Punishment is nothing but this meaningful demonstration. (Durkheim, 1961, p. 166)

In a similar way to Mead, Durkheim in this analysis is arguing that evaluations of punishment which restrict their attention to its effects on individual offenders, as in traditional criminology, are missing its essential meaning. By pointing to the wider social meaning or function of punishment, Durkheim offers a range of hypotheses concerning the relationship between rule violation and punishment which have yet to be investigated by sociologists; for example, in discussing the kind of punishment system a school should set up, he outlines a theory of recidivism which fits well the experience of modern penal systems.

> All punishment, once applied, loses a part of its influence by the very fact of its application. What lends it authority, what makes it formidable, is not so much the misery that it causes as the moral discredit implied in the blame that it expresses. This feeling of moral sensitivity that stands guard against misdeeds is one of the most delicate of sentiments. It is not strong, it is not completely itself, it lacks its full power of influence

71

except among those for whom it has lost nothing of its original purity. We often say that the first offence always leads to others. This is because, once we have felt it, we are less sensitive to this shame. Punishment has this very great limitation of clashing with one of the chief resources of moral life, and thus reducing its own efficacy in the future. It retains all of its force only when it simply constitutes a threat.... Punishment cannot but contribute to future lapses. (Durkheim, 1961, pp. 198-9)

These analyses by Durkheim and Mead of the meaning of deviance and attempts to control it require us to drop our taken-for-granted assumptions about the effects of punishment and draw our attention towards the wider issues of the social meanings attached to laws and their enforcement.

Several American sociologists have developed the implications of Mead's ideas about the peculiar character of punitive justice and have emphasized different aspects. Tannenbaum (1938) refers to the ritual character of the criminal court as the 'dramatization of evil' and sees this very dramatization as contributing to the confirmation of the criminal in his deviant role. In a similar way, Garfinkel calls the court processing of the criminal a 'status degradation ceremony' in which the convicted offender's civil status is dramatically removed and is publicly replaced by the new identity and demoted status of 'criminal' (Garfinkel, 1956).

More recently, Erikson, echoing Durkheim, has pointed out that the very institutions whose ostensible purpose is to correct the deviant seem much more likely to confirm him in his deviant role; our prisons, mental hospitals, borstals and other institutions for those excluded from conventional society provide ample opportunities for learning the 'skills and attitudes of a deviant career, and often

72

provoke them [the excluded] into employing these skills by reinforcing their sense of alienation from the rest of society' (Erikson, 1962). Indeed, in view both of the depressingly, if understandably, high rates of recidivism which the ex-inmates of such institutions produce, and also concomitantly of the miniscule economic and human resources allocated to these institutions, Erikson questions whether we can consider the suppression of deviance to be their 'real' function at all. If we were serious about the suppression of deviance, he asks, would we not devote much more energy and resources to the task? The writings of Tannenbaum, Garfinkel, Erikson and others, then, all rest on Durkheim's and Mead's analyses of crime and society's responses to it, and each of them suggests in complementary ways that the very social processes apparently designed to reduce deviance ironically seem to produce and foster it.

We have now to consider how these complementary views of the normality of crime and deviance can be related to the perspective proposed in the previous chapter. It was suggested that an adequate understanding of crime or any social phenomenon can only come from an investigation of the typical social meanings which individuals give to their situations and out of which they construct their actions. A major task is thus to examine how these typical social meanings emerge, are maintained and change; the individual's consciousness and self-consciousness, his subjectivity, is placed at the centre of this approach, and it is the content of the individual's subjectivity upon which the sociologist draws to build up his patterns of typical social meanings. Clearly the basic unit of study is individual consciousness.

As we have seen, certain ideas about individual consciousness are indispensable to both Durkheim's and Mead's discussions. In Durkheim's analysis at the most fundamental level it is the uniqueness of the individual's consciousness which precludes the possibility of a deviance-free society; moreover, his explanation of how crime, rather than disappearing, only changes its forms, rests on ideas about changing forms of consciousness. The universally experienced heightened sentiment which might rid society of one kind of criminal act serves at the same time to direct the equivalent opprobrium towards acts which previously had only attracted mild disapproval; the change in social consciousness redirects attention and defines new behaviours as criminal. Thus the nature of individual and social consciousness is fundamental to Durkheim's analysis. It is only through shared social meanings that some criminal acts disappear from society and others take their place.

Similarly, Mead's discussion of society's punitive reaction to crime as manifested in the penal system centres on the meanings given to crime and criminals by the members of the community. He shows how the criminal calls forth certain hostile responses and how these responses are crystallized and institutionalized in systems of punitive justice. The social meanings given to criminals and their acts, because of their hostile character, preclude the possibility of nonpunitive methods of treatment based on psychological and sociological understanding of the criminal. Control apparatus reflects the social meaning of crime and the criminal in a given society.

The other authors mentioned all give primacy in their discussions to the forms of consciousness which emerge out of and reinforce our organizational processes for handling the convicted criminal. The ritual and systematic processes of branding, labelling, demoting and excluding the criminal impinge on both the social meanings given to the criminal by members of the community and also, equally importantly, on the social meanings given by the criminal to his own acts and to himself. Such processes arise out of our initial hostility towards the criminal and in their turn effectively reinforce both our hostility and the criminal's view of himself as an outsider. The conscious social meanings thus given to crime and reflected in our systems of handling convicted criminals are all-important for understanding the complementary processes of deviance and control.

The implications of accepting the view that deviance is a normal phenomenon are considerable. Once it is realized that deviance in some form is a fundamental feature of any social group or society, then the analytical problems change accordingly. By accepting the inevitability of deviance, the sociologist's attention is directed away from the search for causes of crime through the study of the biographies of individual convicted criminals and towards social processes and a society's structure of social meanings.

Whilst deviance as a social process is inherent in social organization, this is not to deny that at the individual level there are many different kinds and degrees of deviance which in turn occur for many different reasons. The possible content of deviant processes in a society obviously depends on the structure of formal and informal rules in that society; in complex industrial societies, even if attention is restricted to the range of formal rules, such as the criminal and civil law, they impinge on every area of social life. Given the range of these rules and the situations they relate to, the origins of particular individual deviations are not reducible to a handful of underlying individual characteristics but are as broad as the range of human motivation itself; indeed, the same rule, such as a criminal law, may be broken for polar opposite reasons in different contexts. Shop-lifting may variously be a game for schoolboys, an occupation and livelihood for one adult and an occasional means of saving on the housekeeping expenses for another. Thus, part of the analytical task of the deviance perspective is to clarify the typical social meanings of deviations and to place these in the context of the creation and enforcement of the rule which is being broken.

If deviance is inevitable, if it is inherent in the very nature of society, then to seek to explain it in terms of either individual characteristics or determinate social factors is to blind oneself to its actual nature. Traditional criminology sought to do just that. Its theories and methods were based on the assumption that crime was the result of something within the individual convicted criminal and that by studying the latter eventually the peculiar crime-producing individual characteristics would be located. These characteristics would be the causes, and once they were defined and located society could sift out those individuals who possessed them. Acceptance of the normality of deviance immediately requires a rejection of the traditional view and the substitution of a focus on social processes; it demands a recognition that deviance can only be understood by an examination of the processes of interaction in which some members of a society are labelled as deviant by others and as a result come to take on a deviant identity. This view argues that, while deviance itself is inevitable, the actual patterns of deviance in a society are problematic for the sociologist; it is these patterns which require understanding and not the mere presence of deviance.

In the previous chapter it was suggested that these patterns are composed of typical social meanings; an understanding of crime in any society therefore requires the sociologist to locate both the social meanings which define crime, criminals and social reactions to them in that society and also the processes through which such meanings emerge, change and are maintained.

# 4

# Crime in particular social structures

The discussion in this and the remaining chapters focuses on crime in contemporary industrial societies; the distinctive patterns of crime and societal reactions to them which characterize industrial societies can be understood only by relating them to the surrounding structures of social meaning and social processes. Such structures and processes are very different in character from those which are found in what have traditionally been called simple societies. It is in industrial societies also that particular patterns of criminal behaviour have been publicly defined as 'serious social problems' requiring certain sorts of public action to reduce the problem; we have already noted that this public definition of certain forms of crime and delinquency as important social problems was one of the main reasons why so much time and energy has been directed towards their study by criminologists and sociologists. The ostensibly 'objective' scholars were very much caught up in the value problems of industrial societies. Public definitions of crime as a social problem led to political pressures on such scholars to provide the answers to the 'why' questions about crime and to explicitly or implicitly suggest what might be done about the problem. Thus, overt political interest in crime and delinquency created the conditions in which many scholars chose to undertake research to try and provide answers to the questions of public concern; the amount of time, energy and money spent on the investigation of criminal deviance in a society seems to depend on the quality and scale of crime, the reciprocal strength of public concern with the problem and the amount of money available, as well as the interest and natural curiosity of certain kinds of sociologists.

The confluence of these influences has resulted in an enormous quantity of sociological writing and research on the subject in the United States and comparatively little elsewhere. Thus, a major problem facing analysts from other cultures, such as our own, is how far the vast output of American sociologists contributes to the understanding of crime and delinquency in other societies. Can American theories and data make up for the paucity of these in relation to other industrial societies? Asking this question may help us to distinguish between sociological concepts and data which refer to social processes that are common to industrial societies and those which refer to the peculiar substantive characteristics of one society. In fact the lack of conceptualization and research relating to deviance outside the United States makes it very difficult to draw conclusions about those social phenomena which are common and those which are specific. Nevertheless, the general orienting perspective presented in chapter 2 attempts to direct attention primarily to such common social processes; in particular, these are the processes by which official definitions, and therefore rates of crime and delinquency, emerge from the processes of interaction between the social control mechanisms and some of those individuals who conform to those definitions. The study of the origins, maintenance and consequences of these processes of definition and control were also seen as integral to the deviance perspective. Similarly, the discussion in chapter 3 of the formal processes of social control and the ways in which they define, label and give a specific status to the convicted offender, is also referring to processes common to complex industrial societies. All of them, with slight variations, have developed such public rituals for assigning status to and for punishing convicted offenders. It is these common processes which are considered in more detail in this chapter.

If a concern of the sociologist is to compare similar processes in different societies, in other words, to adopt a comparative perspective, then the empirical study of these processes in different cultures might suggest the ways in which substantive similarities and differences were related to other features of the respective social structures. Unfortunately this kind of comparative study has been almost non-existent in the sphere of social deviance in general and crime and delinquency in particular. It thus becomes rather difficult to fill out the abstract perspective presented in chapter 2 with reliable comparative data. For this reason most of the examples given in the subsequent discussion relate to either the United States, where there has been extensive sociological theorizing and research in the area of social deviance, or to England, where the tradition of investigation has been somewhat different in both quantity and character. While the desirability of ultimately adopting a comparative empirical perspective in sociology should be clear, the difficulties of following this directive currently in the case of social deviance arise from the paucity of reliable comparable empirical investigations.

Sociologists have used a wide variety of concepts for understanding crime and delinquency; similarly, a variety of research methods have been adopted to illustrate some of these concepts and to generate others. Some of the major theoretical and methodological developments in the sociological analysis of crime will be illustrated in the following chapter in which the changing sociological stances towards juvenile delinquency are reviewed. No attempt is made in this chapter to review the conflicting schools of explanation, but rather a series of complementary concepts and ideas, drawn from several authors, are presented. These concepts are intended to provide a relatively integrated approach to the understanding of crime placed within the wider deviance perspective.

However, the point must be made that the concepts used and emphasized in any explanation or piece of research are integral to the nature of the theory proposed and share its assumptions and limitations. Any theory or perspective selects only certain things out of the total situation facing the observer, and what he selects depends on the dominant orienting concepts of the theory; by extension, what is selected out for intensive scrutiny by the investigator will influence considerably the kinds of methods of investigation he uses and therefore ultimately the data which arise from his use of these methods. What this means in practice is that a variety of commonly used sociological concepts such as social class, social role or social structure may be common to different explanations but may be treated very differently in terms of both theory and method in these explanations. In other words, the concepts themselves are given different meanings in different theoretical perspectives; these differences reflect the major internal divisions within sociology over the 'correct' perspective to be adopted in analysing the social world (Winter, 1966). The concepts used by the authors whose work is drawn upon in this chapter are derived mainly from the sociological tradition of subjective interpretation, which broadly comprises Max Weber's *verstehen* sociology, the symbolic interaction of George Herbert Mead and the more recent social phenomenology of Alfred Schuetz; this should be remembered when this discussion is compared to other interpretations.

The first task facing the sociologist who wishes to understand the patterns of crime in a given society is to try to obtain as accurate a picture of these patterns as possible, that is, to describe the main parameters of crime and criminality. Unfortunately, even this basic task of description, a clear prerequisite for analysis, is made very difficult, if not impossible, in the study of crime. The obvious source of data, a society's official criminal statistics, in fact cannot be taken as reliable indices of the amount or quality of illegal behaviour in a society; nor can the officially convicted individuals be taken as a representative sample of all those committing criminal offences. As was pointed out earlier, these were two errors of the traditional approaches to studying crime, although many sociologists continue to commit the first one, probably because of the lack of other accessible data. It is worthwhile examining in more detail the limitations of the official criminal statistics, for it is only through recognizing these limitations that we can decide how, if at all, the sociologist can use such statistics. Similarly, an examination of the nature of the statistics illustrates several important features of the way patterns of deviance emerge and are maintained.

Traditional criminology, by using the criminal law and penal processes to define its subject matter, was placed in the position of limiting its study to those people defined as criminal by a court; its population therefore comprised officially convicted offenders only. Because it was argued that nobody could be seen as a criminal until he had been so defined by a criminal court, the study of those who had not been officially defined was excluded automatically. The complex processes by which some offenders were officially defined as guilty while others were not were taken as given and were seen as non-problematic analytically. The result of official law enforcement procedures, reflected in the official statistical indices of 'persons found guilty' and 'court disposals', were taken as defining the limits of traditional criminology's subject matter. Similarly, the indices relating to offences, especially that of 'crimes known to the police' (hereafter referred to as CKP), were taken as more or less reliable and constant samples, or at least as useful approximations of all criminal offences in society, so that, for example, if the CKP showed a steady rise over a number of years, the traditional tendency was to assume that this reflected a real increase in the number of actual crimes committed in the community. There is still a tendency for this to be done by sociologists who acknowledge the limitations of the CKP index but who justify their use of such official data for this purpose by arguing that there is no alternative and that these are the best data which we have.

The alternative viewpoint proposed here is that with the possible exception of a very small group of offences, indices derived from official data on known criminal offences and offenders are of very little value as measures of the quantity and quality of crime in a society. This does not mean that the official statistics cannot be used usefully by the sociologist but rather that the use he makes of them will be different to that of traditional criminology. A brief examination of some of the statistics' limitations points both to the kinds of uses to which the sociologist may put them and also to some of the important features of crime in industrial societies. Statistics relating to offenders are dealt with first.

There is one general point which both underpins the deviance perspective and also raises the problematic character of the meanings given in our society to the terms 'crime' and 'criminal'. Put succinctly, we are all criminals; there are very few members of our society who have not at some time committed at least one act punishable by a criminal court, and most of us have committed several such crimes. There have been several studies by sociologists of self-reported crimes which show that the vast majority of individuals, when interviewed anonymously, admit to extensive criminal activity. For example, Wallerstein and Wyle (1947) in such a study in the United States found that over 90 per cent of their adult sample admitted to the commission of a range of offences for which they could have been gaoled. The commission of a range of offences seems to be a standard feature of mundane social life in our society; these offences range from what may be considered trivial both in terms of the legal punishments and in public attitudes, such as many traffic offences or forms of minor larceny, to more serious crimes, including various kinds of violence against the person or more serious forms of theft. The ubiquitous character of criminal activity is one further reason for rephrasing the kinds of questions which the sociologist should be asking not only about the official statistics relating to offenders but also about the phenomenon of crime. If everybody commits criminal acts, can we meaningfully look for the 'causes' of crime? Should we not rather be asking why so few people are dealt with by the official mechanisms of social control? If we are all criminal to a degree, do not the key sociological questions concern the processes by which a very small group is selected out and given the official public label of criminal and the effects of such processes? Clearly the social control mechanisms are very highly selective in the legal norms they select for enforcement, in their disposition of organizational resources for control and in whom they actually select out for control. A recognition of the ubiquity both of criminal acts and of criminals (defined simply in terms of those who have committed illegal acts and not in terms of the official decisions

83

of a criminal court) thus raises the importance of the meaning which industrial societies attach to the words 'crime' and 'criminal', for, as was pointed out in the last chapter, one of the major effects of the public rituals in which we process selected criminals is to lead the members of the society to redefine radically the character and identity of those selected.

It would seem most useful, then, to view these official statistics which relate to individual criminals as summary indices of the official selection processes; in other words, any analysis relating to the individuals summed up in the official statistics will tell us more about the nature of the selective social control processes than it will about the quantity and quality of crime in the community (Cicourel and Kitsuse, 1963a). If, as we have suggested, crime comprises all those activities which contravene the wide range of criminal laws within a society, then the official statistics provide us with various indices relating to some of these activities. The index which is typically used to provide a guide to trends in the pattern of criminal activity is the annually produced compilation of 'Crimes known to the police' (CKP); a further index, 'crimes cleared up', is set against this and is often used by politicians, the mass media and the public, as well as the police themselves, as one measure of police efficiency. Both these indices refer to offences and must not be confused with the indices relating to offenders. If data on offenders falls short of providing us with a reliable picture of the community's pattern of criminality, what of the other major statistic relating to offences, that of the CKP?

There are many difficulties involved in interpreting the official criminal statistics as they are currently published; for example, a major limitation is the anachronistic and often misleading division of offences into two groups – 'in-

84

dictable' (the traditionally more serious offences) and 'non-indictable' (the traditionally less serious offences) – for different information is collected about the two groups. The Perks Committee (1967) recommended the abolition of this arbitrary distinction, but their recommendation still awaits implementation. A detailed critique of the current presentation of the official statistics is unnecessary in the present context, but some of their more important general limitations will now be outlined.

In considering the value of the CKP index, two kinds of criteria can be used to differentiate the heterogeneous mass of indictable crimes included. Firstly, offences can be sub-divided according to the nature of the victims; three broad categories of offence can be distinguished in terms of the nature of the victims:

1.  Crimes with identifiable victims, including, e.g., most property offences, all offences against the person;
2.  Crimes without identifiable victims, including mainly consensual crimes and often termed 'vice', e.g. abortion, certain homosexual and heterosexual offences, narcotics offences, gambling offences;
3.  Crimes against the public order or interest, e.g., certain behaviours considered publicly offensive such as drunkenness, traffic offences; various kinds of disorderly behaviour; tax and customs offences.

Some types of crime are clearly difficult to classify according to this criterion; for example, some crimes 'against the State', such as damage to public property, smuggling or tax offences, could be placed in either (2) or (3) above. However, these problems of classification are unimportant in this context.

The second criterion for sub-division concerns the ways

85

in which offences come to be included in the CKP index, and here we encounter the crucial matter of the variability of public values towards offences. Offences come to the notice of the police in two ways: they are either reported by a member or members of the public or they are detected as a result of police initiative and action. The three groups of offences listed above can thus be analysed in the most approximate way in terms of, firstly, their reportability and, secondly, their detectability. When the approximate reportability and detectability for the three offence groups is examined, it becomes clear that there are gross differences between offences in terms of these two qualities and that, as a consequence, the CKP index must be seen as possessing a variable and unknown relation to the actual crimes in society.

Nearly all the known crimes with victims are known because they have been reported by somebody and not because they have been detected initially by the police. In general, this group would seem likely to have higher reportability than the other two categories. However, within this category there are likely to be big differences between offences in reportability. Large-scale property offences, robbery with violence, homicide and other major offences of violence against the person are likely to have high reportability; many minor property offences, especially those carried out within institutional settings such as shops, schools and factories, have low reportability. Reportability is likely to change in an unknown way for any given offence over time and between areas; one cannot assume constant reportability for an offence. Detectability is obviously low, for the police have to rely on victims or others notifying them of an alleged offence. Routine police activitives are confined to publicly accessible spheres, while many crimes with victims – for example, all property crimes by definition – occur in private settings inaccessible to the police in their mundane activity (Stinchcombe, 1963).

The second category, crimes without victims, has very low reportability; perhaps the only kind of reportability which is at all important here is the rather distinctive kind of reporting involved in the police-informer system. But the fact is that nearly all such crimes known to the police are a result of detection; in other words, they arise out of purposive police activity towards these areas of behaviour. This does not mean that they have a high detectability but rather that unless the police went out of their way to detect the few that do appear in the statistics there would be an absence of official data in this sphere. For example, prior to the 1967 Act legalizing abortion under certain conditions, the annual average number of cases of procuring abortion known to the police during the years 1962-6 was 262, whereas unofficial estimates placed the annual figure at something nearer 100,000. In fact the number of crimes of this category known to the police invariably almost equals the number of crimes cleared up by the police, which supports the idea that it is direct police action which detects the offence, the offenders and the evidence at the same time, enabling prosecution to proceed immediately and invariably with success. In the same period, an annual average of 248 cases of procuring abortion were cleared up by the police; between 60 and 70 persons per year were brought to trial for these cases (Home Office, 1967).

The situation is similar with the third category of crimes, those loosely termed 'crimes against the public order'; only a small proportion of these are known to the police as a result of public reporting, the vast majority being known through purposive action by the police. As with the second category, clear-up figures for this group are almost identical with figures of crimes known to the police. Of course, the

87

police only detect a very small minority of those who behave in similar ways; again in the absence of large-scale public reporting of these offences the official figures for public order crimes known and cleared up reflect the nature of differential police organization and activity. Low reportability and low detectability are thus a feature of this third category too. With regard to police activity, a useful distinction is made by Reiss and Bordua in seeing police action as 'reactive' when dealing with crimes with victims, that is, they react to the victims' protests, while for the other two categories they are mainly 'proactive' in that they themselves take the initiative and are responsible for the official crime rates in the second and third categories (Bordua, 1967).

It would seem, then, that it is only within the first group, 'crimes with victims', that official data on a small group of offences may reflect with any accuracy the patterns of offences in the community. Even for these carefully selected groups of offences, the kinds of comparisons which both the sociologist and the public want to make, such as the examination of trends over time, may not be viable because of the unknown influences which changes in public reporting habits, in police organization and sometimes in the law may have on what gets into the official data.

According to the official criminal statistics for England and Wales and studies of officially convicted offenders, the official picture of crime is one of a criminal population comprised mainly of young working-class males whose criminal activity is concerned chiefly with property, violence and a wide range of offences associated with the motor car. The official figures of CKP show a steady rise in numbers since 1956 for the main groups of offences, with a few exceptions. In fact the proportionate increases have varied considerably between offences: property offences

CKP (larceny, breaking and entering) have risen by almost three times in the twelve years from 1956, while the number of offences of violence has more than trebled; sexual offences in the same period rose by about a third (Home Office, 1969). The motor car, property and the person are the focal points of official crime in our society and these focal points are common to most industrial societies, although the official levels and patterns vary considerably between societies.

Cross-cultural differences are well illustrated in the case of homicide, the official figures for which are likely to be more reliable than most other criminal statistics. Wolfgang and Ferracuti (1967), in presenting the case for a sub-cultural explanation of violence, provide statistics which show that there are big differences between industrial societies in their homicide rates; among these societies, the United States, with a rate in 1960 of 4·5 homicides per 100,000 of the population, has a much higher rate than Japan (1·9 per 100,000), France (1·7 per 100,000), Italy (1·4 per 100,000), England and Wales (0·6 per 100,000) or the Netherlands (0·3 per 100,000). The fact that the United States has an official homicide rate over seven times that of England and Wales suggests one of the reasons why our main source of theories about and research into crime is the United States. Official rates for property and violence offences in the United States are also well ahead of those in other industrial societies, although as we have suggested these are much less reliable than the homicide figures and must be treated only as minimum estimates. However, other kinds of evidence suggest that the scale of property theft is altogether different to that in this country. In Manhattan, property theft is so common that many householders and flat occupants find it impossible to insure their belongings against theft.

It seems, then, that while we do get a picture of the patterns of offences and offenders from the official statistics, the differences in reportability and detectability of offences and offenders place clear limits on the uses to which such statistics can be put. The use of CKP as a guide to the patterns of crime in society and changes and trends in this statistic over time must be treated with the greatest scepticism.

In fact the problem is confounded when police clear-up rates are examined, that is, the proportion of crimes known which the police clear up to their own satisfaction. As mentioned, there are big differences between offences; but taking the two main groups of property offences, in England and Wales in 1968 offences against property with violence had a clear-up rate of 36 per cent, offences against property without violence had one of 41 per cent, whereas one of the more common offences of violence against the person, malicious wounding, had a clear-up rate of 81 per cent (Home Office, 1969). In the United States the overall clear-up rate for crimes known to the police is about 25 per cent (Savitz, 1967). Clearly the odds are on the side of the offender. Given this situation, it should be clear that to do as traditional criminology and sociology did in searching for the causes of crime by studying those individuals selected out by the social control agencies, obviously a minority of all offenders, was a fundamental error.

It does not follow, however, that because of these limitations the official criminal statistics are of no interest or value to the sociologist, but rather that the limitations do require that a different perspective be adopted towards them. Firstly, the statistics provide an indication of the rules which a society, through the interpretations of the enforcers, feels it is important to enforce at any point in time and minimum estimations of deviations from these

90

rules; only a handful of these estimations – for example, that for murder – are likely to approximate the actual numbers of deviations from given rules.

Secondly, two areas are suggested for investigation: the reporting of offences by the public and police activity in detection and law enforcement; so far sociologists who have worked more or less within this perspective, such as Skolnick (1966) and Cicourel (1968), have concentrated almost entirely on studying police activity and have clarified the ways in which features of police organization, their relationships with the community and their interaction with offenders contribute to the production of official crime rates. Studies of reporting are less developed and we have only a hazy understanding of differential reporting practices (e.g., Martin, 1962).

Thirdly, while recognizing that statistics relating to convicted offenders should be viewed mainly as indices of official action, nevertheless official action may locate areas or neighbourhoods in which certain kinds of law-breaking are fairly common and where there are high concentrations of official criminals and delinquents. The well-established sociological finding that some neighbourhoods have high official crime rates while other adjacent and similar neighbourhoods have low official crime rates is of interest to the sociologist, and the alternative perspective suggested in chapter 2 would considerably widen the scope of sociological investigation into such differences. For example, it would be as important to examine the standard police methods of locating suspects as it would be to study the social meanings which the officially criminal population attached to their delinquent activities. However, the problems of identifying the unofficial criminals in the 'low rate' or the 'high rate' areas are likely to be as great for the sociologist as for the police, for obvious reasons. Similarly, the statistics may occasionally provide an unexpected bonus by directing attention to previously ignored phenomena. An example of this would be the recent finding in a study of delinquency in an inner London borough that there were vast differences in the official delinquency rates of overtly similar secondary schools within the borough (Phillipson, 1971).

Fourthly, those criminal statistics which relate to the processing of detected offenders, that is, those which summarize court actions towards offenders, can be useful indices of trends in official control practices. In other words, consistencies or changes in court practices can be examined, for example in relation to the changing use of prison, probation or fining for different groups of offenders.

Finally, the implications of this way of looking at the official statistics for the questions asked by sociologists are radical and relate to the discussion of the normality of crime in chapter 3. If crime is a normal phenomenon, if most members of society commit criminal acts either occasionally or frequently and if, as the statistics show, many offences carry low expectations of conviction, should we be asking not why is there so much official crime, but why is there so little? Similarly, should we ask not why those who did get caught committed their offences, but rather how so many people 'get away with it' and what are the effects of not 'getting away with it' for the caught offenders and the community? Once again, these questions take us back to the relationships between the 'law-abiding public', the official offenders, the unofficial offenders and the agencies of social control.

These, then, are some of the limitations and the possibilities of the official descriptive data on crime and criminals. The first apparent task of the sociologist, that of describing accurately the quantitative and qualitative dimensions of crime, is thus seen to be ruled out by the impossibility of accurately measuring crime in the community; if the descriptive task is not possible, this would seem to call into question any interpretations or theories of crime causation which are founded initially on such inadequate data. Clearly the sociologist, whatever his theoretical stance, cannot explain or interpret adequately any phenomenon which he cannot initially describe. Any such explanations become either gross distortions of reality or so divorced from reality that they seem to be vacuous rhetoric directed to other sociologists. Explanations of both kinds have appeared with disappointing frequency in criminology and sociology.

The alternative social deviance perspective at least has the virtue that the phenomena with which it is concerned are potentially describable and hence sociologically understandable; they are open to sociological investigation although not necessarily of the conventional kind. Description of certain social processes within which deviance emerges does seem to be possible, and this enables the sociologist to offer an interpretation. In particular, his interpretations will generally be directed to showing the relationship between the criminal or deviant phenomena which he describes and other social processes which may appear initially to have little to do with deviance. The unconventional can only be understood by seeing how it is inextricably intertwined with the conventional. The rest of this chapter is concerned with the kinds of questions which the sociologist might ask in trying to describe and understand criminal deviance; three American sociologists who have made significant contributions to the sociological analysis of deviance – Becker, Matza and Lemert – provide the main orienting concepts.

Whilst it may be a truism, it is certainly true to say that

there can be no deviance and therefore no crime without rules. Perhaps it is the painfully obvious character of this statement which accounts in part for the almost total refusal of sociologists to take any notice of its implications until very recently. Howard Becker, in *Outsiders*, is the first sociologist to have made explicit some of these implications. In his words:

> ... social groups create deviance by making the rules whose infraction constitutes deviance, and by applying those rules to particular people and labelling them as outsiders. From this point of view, deviance is *not* a quality of the act the person commits, but rather a consequence of the application by others of rules and sanctions to an 'offender'. The deviant is one to whom that label has successfully been applied; deviant behaviour is behaviour that people so label. (Becker, 1963, p. 9)

In fact, Becker distinguishes between rule-breaking behaviour, by which he means those rule infractions which have not been successfully sanctioned by society (e.g., the unidentified criminal law-breaker) and deviant behaviour, that is, those behaviours which have been labelled and sanctioned as such by others.

In making this distinction Becker is suggesting that a recognition of the process of labelling someone a deviant following his commission of a given act may be crucial for an understanding of his subsequent rule-breaking. This point will be taken up in looking at Lemert's contribution. However, in drawing attention to the rules which are created and enforced at the societal level, Becker is pointing to a sphere previously ignored by most sociologists of deviance, that of politics. The criminal laws of complex industrial societies are generated in the political sphere, and the actual form in which any given law emerges is usually

94

the result of a long process of argument between conflicting interest groups. The law resulting from such conflict is likely to be very much of a compromise between the different interest groups and not necessarily representative of one particular standpoint. A recent example of such compromise in England would be the Homicide Act of 1957, which drew the distinction between capital and non-capital murder in an attempt to satisfy both the retentionists and the abolitionists. Similarly, the Act of 1967 which widened the conditions in which abortion could be legally performed was the result of much bitter disagreement between organized pressure groups such as the Roman Catholic Church, sections of the medical profession and the Abortion Law Reform Association. The resulting law seemed very much of a compromise and open to many different interpretations. Becker is thus suggesting that the rules of a society may reflect the particular interests of those in a society who are in a position to create and then to ensure the attempted enforcement of these rules; these groups or individuals are referred to by Becker as 'moral entrepreneurs'. The rule creators are, typically, moral crusaders concerned with certain highly valued ends which usually involve translating a general value into a specific rule or law. The specific laws are drawn up by the professionals, typically lawyers, and it is they who are responsible for fitting the new law into the existing web of legislation; they too have values which may enter into the framing of the rule.

The enforcement of the new rule may require a new body of enforcers, as in the case of factory legislation, or it may be placed in the hands of the existing enforcers, typically the police. To the latter, rule enforcement is a job, and the enforcers initially may have little interest in the actual content of the law; where the enforcers' interests do not centre in the content of the rule but rather in the techniques of enforcement, there is considerable latitude for them to develop their own scale of priorities of enforcement. Whilst these priorities are subject to external pressures from the rule creators, the politicians, the mass media or the public directly, the discretion of the enforcers is considerable; they thus develop informal rules and methodical techniques for enforcing the formal rules. The official criminal statistics are a result of the consistent application of these informal rules. From Becker's point of view, then, deviance and those labelled as deviant must be seen as :

> ... a consequence of a process of interaction between people, some of whom in the service of their own interests make and enforce rules which catch others, who in the service of their own interests, have committed acts which are labelled deviant. (Becker, 1963)

By pointing out that the creation of rules is a political act, Becker calls into question the consensual quality of the criminal law and forces us to ask whose interests any given body of law represents. One immediate question would be : are there any areas of criminal law which would attract universal agreement or consensus? The only certain answer to this is that there is consensus about those laws which have fallen into disuse for a variety of reasons. Empirically there is obviously no consensus because everybody is involved in some kind of rule-breaking intermittently. Yet the problem of consensus can be looked at in another way, and it is a way which suggests that Becker may have overdrawn slightly the picture of conflict and disagreement over rule creation and enforcement.

If, as Becker suggests, rules are created and maintained as a result of the processes of pressure group politics, one can examine those areas of the criminal law which continue to be enforced, however selectively, but which do not seem to have attracted the attention of a reforming pressure group; two areas stand out as having been largely untouched by such groups: offences against the person and offences against private property. There have certainly been and still are reform groups whose concern is to change what is done in the name of society to offenders in both these groups, and changes in the forms of punishment have been effected as a result of their pressures; but any organization which has taken place on the other side of the law in these areas has been directed not at changing the law but at breaking it. Perhaps at this point it is useful to refer back to Mead's analysis which was summarized in the previous chapter. Although he did not specify the crimes to which he was referring, his analysis seems most pertinent in relation to crimes with victims; members of the community, in developing and accepting the ritual public processing and punishing of criminals, symbolically place themselves in the role of the victim and his or her relations. Taking the role of the victim creates a recognition of the identity of interests of self and victim; the self-interests, whether protection of property or body, are similar to those of the victim. This recognition leads to an acceptance of the legitimacy of law and punishment in such areas of behaviour; in this case the sociological problem becomes one of understanding how individual offenders neutralize the moral bind of the law in particular situations enabling them to victimize another. The tacit agreement of both the regular rule breakers and rule keepers to the continued enforcement of the laws which outlaw crimes with victims seems to reflect the taken-for-granted belief that the rule breaker stands to lose as much as the rule keeper by the abolition of these laws. Indeed, the small number of political parties and groups which currently publicly advocate the

97

abolition of private property do not, as far as we know, actually put their beliefs regarding other people's property into extensive practice in the present society; but they do involve themselves publicly in the political process and openly attempt to convert others to their cause. This seems to be the antithesis of the mundane property rule breaker, who neither seems to desire change of the property laws nor to attempt to convert the public to mass property theft. Similarly, the laws creating offences of violence against the person do not seem to have attracted any noticeable abolitionist movement, although the proponents of some political ideologies often seem dangerously close to advocating the legitimacy of such violence in certain circumstances.

The processes of rule creation and differential rule enforcement, then, are the background against which any further study of deviance must be set; indeed, the role of moral entrepreneurs in these processes would seem particularly important in relation to the rules creating crimes without victims and crimes against the public order. Becker confines his examples to such crimes, the rules for which seem much more open to changes than crimes with victims. A more detailed discussion of these and other issues concerning crimes without victims is presented by Schur (1965).

The other side of law-making is also important in this context; those laws and public orders which define what is to be done to the offender once found guilty not only are a result of and subject to the same sorts of political processes, but they are also closely bound up with the deviance-producing processes in a society. If a society changes the ways in which it decides to deal with certain groups of offenders, the changes will have unintended consequences which will be reflected in subsequent patterns of deviance. The arguments of Erickson and others concerning the effects of penal institutions, together with the rates of recidivism following institutionalization, suggest that any changes in the patterns of use of penal institutions (such as the introduction of the detention centre following the 1948 Criminal Justice Act) will have unknown effects on the levels of rule-breaking and deviance; in view of the evidence, it seems most unlikely that an increase in either the use of existing institutions or in the creation of new ones will do anything other than increase the amount of rule-breaking in the community. A recent piece of legislation making fundamental changes in the ways in which our society deals with juvenile and young offenders, the Children and Young Persons Act of 1969, will have an unknown effect on the official figures relating to juvenile delinquency because it changes radically the relationship between the police and the juvenile offender; similarly, the Act proposes major and long-term changes in the pattern of institutions for juvenile offenders which, when developed, will undoubtedly play a considerable, although largely unknowable, part in the dynamics of juvenile deviance. Thus it is not only changes in the criminal law which are important in defining the limits of deviance but also changes in any part of the social control apparatus which a society has developed to deal with deviants; many of the organizations explicitly concerned with social welfare may be seen as parts of a society's social control apparatus, so that the variety of sources of direct influence on deviance is considerable.

We have seen that in accepting the normality of crime the sociologist's attention is drawn towards issues other than the 'causes' of crime; thus, in interpreting the pattern of crime presented in the official statistics, his problem is one of seeing the production of such statistical rates as the outcome of a complex joint enterprise rather than as a reflection of actual crime in the community. The word normality also suggests another feature of crime; far from being extraordinary, most officially processed crime is rather ordinary and generates little excitement or interest; it is ordinary in part because it happens all the time. A crime has to be both unusual in its character and relatively rare in its commission to arouse the interest and passions of many members of the society; when they do occur, such crimes are invariably given much attention in the mass media. Ordinary crimes are by and large left to the local press to report selectively.

Focusing on the mundane character of most crime points to a further feature of rule-breaking in our society which was first made explicit by David Matza (1964) in *Delinquency and Drift*. Opposing the traditional positivist perspective which had continually sought but signally failed to demonstrate how different criminals were to the law-abiding members of the community, Matza argued that the key to understanding delinquency was to recognize how closely it was integrated with the surrounding culture. Far from being separate from or the antithesis of 'conventional' culture, the culture of delinquency, and by extension much crime, could only be understood by a recognition not of its differences from but of its similarities and integration with the surrounding social world.

We have seen that rule-breaking, including criminal rule-breaking, is very common in our culture; there are few individuals who do not contravene – some of them frequently – rules that are publicly sanctionable. Yet, typically, much of this rule-breaking is not viewed as crime by the actors; for many acts, such as stealing from work, there exists a series of justifications and beliefs which renders application of the term 'crime' apparently redundant because the actors themselves and the rule enforcers share the belief that such acts are all right under the circumstances. The meaning of the act changes according to the situation; where there is a reasonable coincidence in the beliefs of the actor, the victim and the enforcer that a given act is not really a crime (or perhaps that it is not a crime worth bothering about, which amounts in practice to the same thing), then the meaning of the word 'crime' itself is called into question. The mutual unspoken agreements to treat given acts as 'all right under the circumstances' or only as privately rather than publicly sanctionable, suggests the need for empirical rather than abstract definitions of crime; this means recognizing that the universality of rule-breaking is attended by extensive particularism in the definition of crime through rule enforcement. The breaking of criminal laws seems to be an extension or reflection of the rule-breaking which is a continuing feature of conventional social processes. There is no clear-cut line that can be drawn between rule-breaking of a non-criminal kind and breaking the criminal law.

A further feature of Matza's discussion reinforces the view of integration rather than separation. In looking at the values which are expressed in juvenile delinquency, Matza argues that, far from being the antithesis of conventional culture, as many have argued, they seem to be extensions, exaggerations or sometimes badly-timed expressions of quite ordinary values. Excitement, masculinity and a distaste for mundane work are the values reflected in ordinary male delinquency and are also values shared in common with most male members of society; Matza argues that these are typically regarded as 'leisure values' in conventional culture. The surrounding culture, however, expresses these values in somewhat different ways in typically non-delinquent, although often morally marginal, situations.

Again, similarity and not difference expresses the relationship between some of the typical juvenile rule breakers' values and some of those expressed by the surrounding community.

A third feature of ambiguity about rule-breaking in our society can be found in the area defined by E. H. Sutherland (1949) as 'white-collar crime'; he was referring to the rule-breaking of those in high status occupations in the course of their work, although he actually narrowed the field down in his own investigations to the study of offences committed by business organizations. Governments create many laws to control business activity; these relate to such things as the control of monopoly development, false advertising, various forms of taxation, working conditions and many others. In only a few of these areas is rule-breaking liable to criminal prosecution, as most such activity falls under the aegis of the civil law or administrative regulations of various kinds. Punishments for such rule-breaking are qualitatively different from those meted out by the criminal courts, usually taking the form of fines or orders to 'cease and desist' the particular rule-breaking activity. The strength of government inspection and control is often weak, and the kinds of policing necessary to control adequately this kind of activity do not seem to have been attempted by governments in capitalist societies. It is comparatively easy, therefore, for business organizations to break many of these rules, since their enforcement invariably lacks teeth.

In some senses these offences are rather similar to crimes against the public order, because the official regulations typically outlaw the activities as being 'against the public interest'; nevertheless, the organizations are processed very differently by the community. The lack of interest of the public in such offences may stem to a considerable extent from the fact that they are treated so differently; the crucial feature of public stigmatization and the processes of status and identity change inherent in our penal processes are remarkably absent from our kid-glove handling of delinquent business enterprises. Moreover, the values which such activities represent may not be very different from what is actually applauded as 'good business' in society. It seems to be very difficult to draw a line between what is defined as good business practice and offences against the public interest; many such offences may actually be justified therefore as simply minor modifications of the business ethic. But however such infractions are justified by the individuals in the organizations who are responsible, the differential character of law enforcement and punishment suggests a double standard of law enforcement, one for the individual and one for the organization; they also reflect both the considerable ambivalence and uncertainty in our society about the role of law and punishment and the prevalence of institutionalized rule-breaking. Thus, noting the extensive character of organizational offences and their acceptance and tolerance by public and enforcement agencies, together with the fact that those responsible are generally regarded as the backbone of conventional culture, reinforces Matza's emphasis on the similarities rather than the differences between criminal rule breakers and the surrounding culture.

Another feature of rule-breaking in conventional culture which did not directly concern Sutherland but which would be relevant to Matza's point and of interest to the sociologist of deviance would be professional malpractice. Occupational groups which attempt to be exclusive by controlling entry to the occupation are expanding rapidly in our society; the older professions, such as medicine and the law, are being joined by newer ones modelling themselves on similar lines. Their work is generally one involving the provision of some services for a client, and the nature of the relationship between the professional and a client can be open to various sorts of exploitation and manipulation; apart from governmental regulation, which is often difficult to invoke if the client does not know his rights, the professions attempt to police themselves. In other words, care is taken to prevent knowledge of professional malpractice getting outside the profession because of the possible damage to the reputation of the profession. As in the case of mundane criminal offences, we must presume that the handful of cases of professional malpractice which are publicly dealt with, such as the gross negligence of a doctor in an operation, forms only the tip of a large iceberg of professional rule-breaking. Thus, those professions with the highest prestige and the most developed forms of organization are in the best position to provide immunity from law enforcement for their delinquent members.

Having emphasized the common character of rule-breaking, the difficulty of drawing clear lines between criminal and non-criminal activity and the consequent integration of deviance with conventional culture, the processes through which some deviants are selected out and their consequences can now be examined, for it is as a result of these processes that any separation which does not exist between deviant and conventional worlds seems to arise. The distinction drawn by Lemert (1951) between primary deviation and secondary deviation provides an orientation to these processes.

Lemert proposes that the study of deviation must distinguish between two broad categories of deviation with distinctive aetiologies. Firstly, there is that which he terms 'primary deviation'; this category includes the *original* 'causes' or reasons for an individual's first deviant acts.

104

These primary reasons for the first deviant acts are likely to be almost as heterogeneous as the situations in which deviance can occur; we have suggested in this chapter that the vast majority of the population intermittently commits criminal acts, and the enormous range of situations in which these acts occur preclude any simple explanations of their origins. Explanations for this range of activity would have to sub-divide the field extensively and would require situational analyses of these early rule-breaking acts. Lemert's main point, however, regarding primary deviation is that these first acts, whether tentative and probing or calculated and unambiguous, are unlikely to have profound effects on the individual's beliefs about himself; the typical response is for the actor to view the initial deviant act as a minor aberration justifiable under the circumstances and bearing little relation to his estimate of the sort of person he 'really' is. The act or acts become, in Lemert's words: 'merely troublesome adjuncts of normally conceived roles' (Lemert, 1951, p. 75). Lemert refers to the process by which the actor fits the commission of the deviant act into his existing conception of himself as 'normalization'; this normalization is often supported culturally in a variety of ways. Deviance at this stage is viewed therefore as a normal variation of everyday behaviour, which has 'only marginal implications for the psychic structure of the individual', and the deviations remain primary 'as long as they are rationalized or otherwise dealt with as functions of a socially acceptable role' (Lemert, 1951, p. 75).

The limitation of deviations to this stage hinges crucially on the reactions of other people, which may be expressed in varying strengths of moral indignation, and in particular on the reaction of formal social control agencies. The form which these reactions take may create moral and practical problems for the deviant actor to resolve; particular problems for the criminal deviant arise from the stigmatization, the punishments, the segregation and other forms of social control which he may experience in response to his primary rule-breaking acts. If the responses of others to the primary deviation effectively differentiate, either symbolically or actually, the deviant from his normal milieu, this creates moral problems for him which require resolution. When these problems are resolved, either partially or completely, by subsequent deviation, Lemert classifies these later acts as secondary deviation. The intensity and formality of society's controlling reactions to deviation and their consequent stigmatizing effect become of central importance for the deviant. The more severe the controlling reaction, the more difficult it becomes for him to normalize his deviation; he is required to reassess its meaning for himself and to undertake some self-reorganization. There seem to be two general directions which this reorganization can take: firstly, the individual may adopt another normal role, either abandoning his deviant actions altogether or finding a more tolerated form of deviance; secondly, he may move towards the assumption of a deviant role. Lemert says of the second alternative: 'When a person begins to employ his deviant behaviour or a role based upon it as a means of defence, attack or adjustment to the overt and covert problems created by the consequent societal reaction to him, his deviation is secondary' (Lemert, 1951, p. 76).

In fact, the fully-fledged secondary deviant, the person whose 'life and identity are organised around the facts of deviance', is only likely to emerge from a progressive sequence of interactions between himself as deviant and the social controllers, in which societal reactions compound the development of the deviant's emerging identity. The secondary deviant is one for whom his deviant status is of primary importance.

106

Lemert suggests the likely sequential process, comprising a series of stages, out of which the secondary deviant emerges. A similar scheme has been proposed subsequently by Wilkins (1964), who terms it a 'deviation-amplification system'. Both schema see the individual emerging with a deviant identity out of a progressive sequence of inter-actions between the deviants and the social controllers. Initial deviance leads to segregation, which leads to more deviance, which in turn leads to more severe punishments, which lead to yet more deviance, and so on, perhaps *ad infinitum*. The deviants, progressively excluded, come to de-velop identities which centre on the deviant status and life styles to match.

The distinction made by Lemert between primary and secondary deviation occurs in a more general discussion of social control in which he also distinguishes between active and passive social control. The latter refers to an aspect of conformity to traditional norms, while active social control is a process for the implementation of goals and values. Active social control, as mentioned earlier, is extremely variable in terms both of the values chosen for implementa-tion and also of the forms of implementation and is subject to a variety of pressures; because of this variability, Lemert argues, it is meaningless to talk in abstract terms about 'delinquency' for that activity which becomes known as 'delinquent' and those individuals whom we refer to as 'delinquents' only arise out of the complex processes of interaction between the active social controllers and se-lected rule breakers. It seems clear, he argues, that ' "de-linquency" in our society has no substantive meaning in a sense of a form or essence of behaviour which can be described independently of judgments and symbolically coloured reactions of others to it' (Lemert, 1967, p. 25). He therefore proposes that the sociologist should study the

107

processes and contexts in which delinquent meanings are attached officially and unofficially to a variety of behaviours, for it is in such processes that deviant identities are assigned and emerge.

Becker provides the final orienting concept for this discussion in his use of the term 'career' and the allied notion of personal 'commitment' to the career. Career usually refers to an individual's pattern of movement in his occupation and certain kinds of commitment are prerequisites for 'progress' in the career; similarly, there may be typical contingencies or stages in any particular occupational career which are seen as indicators of such progress by those inside and outside the occupation. Becker (1963) argues that the career analogy offers useful insights into the processes of transition from normal to deviant status, the emergence of a deviant identity and the entry into a deviant group or world. The analogy may have limitations if it is applied indiscriminately to all forms of deviance, as Lemert (1967) has pointed out, but when applied to the sequence of experiences of many delinquents and criminals, it sensitizes us to important features of the emergence and maintenance of deviant identities and groups.

Initially, the contrast might be drawn between those who flirt with delinquency or crime on a casual basis and then drift back into convention and those who follow up their initial flirtation with progressive involvement in crime. For example, a study of juvenile delinquency in East London found that about 50 per cent of boys who appear before a juvenile court do not reappear before a court while they are juveniles (Power, 1965); this would seem to be a useful starting point for examining the juvenile careers of selected boys from the two groups. Of obvious importance in this example would be how the juveniles were selected for formal rather than informal action in the first place and the nature of the interaction between them and the social control agencies both at first court appearance and subsequently.

The idea of commitment directs attention to those who continue their rule-breaking activities over a considerable period and who increasingly see themselves as deviant; deviance becomes, if not the main activity around which their life is organized, at least of continuing importance in the way it impinges on other activities and relationships. Becker argues – and there is a good deal of evidence to support this – that typically deviant motives are socially learned in interaction with other rule breakers; very often sub-cultures emerge which are either organized around particular kinds of deviant activity or identity, or for whose members certain kinds of deviance are recurrent activities and are comfortably integrated with other group activities. Thus a major concern of sociologists in the field of deviance in general and crime and delinquency in particular has been in the varying forms of group support for deviant activities. It is obviously not suggested that group support is a necessary condition of either initial or continued individual rule-breaking, but rather that this is a typical concomitant of much deviance, and one which contributes to the building and maintenance of individual deviant identities. In fact, two studies of particular groups of criminals point to the opposite feature, that of isolation from other deviants as being a concomitant of the criminal enterprise: Cressey's study of embezzlers (Cressey, 1953) and Lemert's study of naïve cheque-forgers (Lemert, 1958) both established that these offences were typically committed in isolation from other criminals. The individual forger or embezzler developed his own justifications for the act. These studies, coupled with the immense variety of possible criminal deviations, suggest that it is certainly possible to undertake both initial and continued deviance without group support, but whether a deviant identity emerges and is sustained will depend very much on other people's definition of the rule breaker. The question of sub-culture will be considered in more detail in the next chapter in relation to juvenile delinquency.

Like the other writers, Becker gives considerable importance to the contribution of the labelling process to the building up of a deviant identity. The process, discussed by Garfinkel (1956), by which the status degradation of the criminal law breaker publicly takes place, results in the imputation of a 'master status' by others to the deviant; whereas previously the individual may have been to others, first and foremost, a 'reliable clerk', a 'lazy husband' or a 'quiet neighbour', he is seen after the public ceremony as 'after all really a thief'. Not only do others now change their behaviour towards him, they also typically reinterpret his past biography as leading up to this deviant act 'all along'; his past life is examined and clues sought which will 'explain' and confirm his deviant character. In other words, retrospectively he is seen as having been 'essentially' a thief all the time; his deviant act, viewed retrospectively, is seen as the natural culmination of his 'real', 'underlying' identity.

This imputation of identity is associated, too, with what Becker calls the generalized symbolic value, which one deviant trait or act is given by others; this is the tendency of others to assume that the actor possesses other undesirable traits which they believe are associated with the new label or status. A thief is assumed to possess generalized dishonesty and is certainly viewed as likely to do the same sort of thing again; others may fill out their picture of him by imputing other sorts of personal characteristics to him also. This is the process of stereotyping; from a few isolated biographical details a generalized picture is built up of the individual. Inevitably the stereotype of the deviant is unfavourable, for the 'evils' of his particular deviance are commonly held to have been produced by other preceding 'evils' in his character. Another area of deviance in which people behave largely on the basis of stereotypes is that of mental disorder; there is a wide variety of labels (such as 'nutcase', 'loony', 'cracked', 'off his head', 'round the bend', etc.) which are symbolically attached to people defined as mentally ill, and the substantive meanings given to such labels may bear little relation to the labelled person's actual behaviour. Nevertheless, people typically behave towards the labelled person not on the basis of his actual behaviour but in terms of their stereotype of him. Scheff (1966), in his book *Being Mentally Ill*, has an interesting discussion of the conventional stereotypes found in the everyday verbal and visual imagery used in relation to mental illness.

In fact, as Goffman (1963), Wilkins (1964) and others have pointed out, in the comparatively anonymous urban settings in which many of our day-to-day contacts with others are of an impersonal nature, we invariably behave towards others on the basis of stereotypes; the others with whom we have fleeting meetings are treated as representatives of categories rather than as individuals. Now, for most of the time, this presents no real problems; some may not enjoy the depersonalization, but at least it facilitates our interaction with others. But when we behave towards deviants in this way, because the generalized symbolic value of our stereotypes typically imputes other 'evil' attributes, the implications may be more serious, especially for the deviant himself. As he builds his identity in interaction with others and, as important, others behave towards him consistently in terms of the generalized stereotype, so he has to take their imputations constantly into account. As it is central to other people in their dealings with him, so it perforce becomes central for him. In Becker's words: 'the deviant identification becomes the controlling one' (Becker, 1963). The difficulties of side-stepping a deviant identity and therefore of discontinuing deviant activity may be considerable under these circumstances. Jean Genet, in his autobiographical *The Thief's Journal*, illustrates this particular aspect in the emergence of his own rather special deviant identity during his stay at the Mettray Reformatory; his responses to others' imputations are vividly described.

> In order to become a colonist, as the children [in the reformatory] were called, I had to force myself. Like most of the little hoodlums, I might spontaneously, without giving thought to them, have performed the many actions which *realize the colonist*. I would have known naïve joys and sorrows; life would have offered me only trivial thoughts, those which anyone could utter. Mettray, which gratified my amorous taste to the full, always wounded my sensibility. I suffered there. I felt the cruel shame of having my head shaved, of being dressed in unspeakable clothes, of being confined in that vile place; I knew the contempt of the other colonists who were stronger or more malicious than I. In order to weather my desolation when I withdrew more deeply into myself, I worked out, without meaning to, a rigorous discipline. The mechanism was somewhat as follows (I have used it since): to every charge brought against me, unjust though it be, from the bottom of my heart I shall answer yes. Hardly had I uttered the word – or the phrase signifying it – than I felt within me the need to become what I had been accused of being. I was sixteen years old. The reader has understood: I kept no place in my heart where the feeling of innocence might take shelter. I owned to being the coward, traitor, thief and fairy they saw in me. An accusation can be made with-

out proof, but it will seem that in order to be found guilty I must have committed the acts which make traitors, thieves or cowards; but this was not at all the case: within myself, with a little patience, I discovered, through reflection, adequate reason for being named by these names. And it staggered me to know that I was composed of impurities. I became abject. Little by little I grew used to this state. I openly admit it. (Genet, 1964, pp. 175-6)

A further important stage in the deviant career which reinforces the deviant's self-concept is entry into an organized group of deviants. The deviant group tends to develop an ideology, just as do other professions and occupations, which justify the members' past activities and give them rationales or vocabularies of motive (Mills, 1963b) for continuing their deviance in the future. As well as these justifications, the deviant also finds solutions to the problems of being deviant already worked out for him; others have faced problems of stigmatization, of dealing with the police or with relations, and they provide him with a range of solutions which facilitates his handling of the problems. Clearly, once the individual has thoroughly absorbed the deviant group's view of the world, the barriers to moving away from the group and adopting conventional world views become considerable; indeed, the incentive for such a move may be low, for the deviant group's ideology and supports must be viewed not simply in negative terms but also in terms of the positive satisfactions and rewards which accrue from membership. It is not the case that individuals maintain such groups only because they have to, but, to a considerable extent, they do so because their rewards are experienced as emotionally satisfying, and certainly as more satisfying than the circumstances of the lone, isolated deviant. Similarly, to reiterate Matza's argument, deviant groups, with their apparently distinctive styles, can only be understood in terms not of their separation from the conventional culture but of their integration within it; such groups are completely circumscribed by the conventional culture and owe any identity which they possess to their ongoing relationships with conventional folk.

Finally, it is worth re-emphasizing that the move back into the conventional world is hindered by the once-for-all character of the deviant status. As Erickson (1962) points out, we have elaborate rituals for giving this status to individuals, but we have nothing comparable for removing it and reinstating them to their conventional civil status. The ex-convict may justifiably feel that he has paid society's price at the end of his prison sentence, but that is not the way society generally, nor the law enforcers themselves, see it; he remains for others a suspect person likely to re-offend, and others' behaviour towards him constantly reminds him of this (Matza, 1969).

The career analogy, then, with its associated ideas of commitment and career stages or contingencies, usefully directs our attention to issues which seem relevant to an understanding of the emergence of deviant identities.

In this chapter we have suggested that if the sociologist's task is one of description and interpretation, then the scope of traditional criminological and sociological perspectives on crime is both expanded and changed if the deviance perspective is adopted. At the descriptive stage the scope is widened by recognizing the inadequacy of official statistics as reliable guides to the patterns of law-breaking in society; the requirement, therefore, is both to describe the variable processes in which the official statistics are constructed and also to describe those situations in which some persistent rule breakers are assured of immunity from enforcement and stigmatization. In both of these cases attention is drawn, firstly, to the processes of interaction between the public, the rule breakers and the rule enforcers and, secondly, to the typical meanings through which these interaction patterns are sustained. It was suggested that these processes, once described, can only be understood by placing them in the wider political context of rule creation and enforcement. Similarly, the emergence within individuals of deviant identities and their frequent attachment to deviant groups can be understood as a response called out by the alienating and isolating reactions of social audiences to their primary deviations. In the next chapter the sociological analysis of juvenile delinquency is taken to illustrate in more detail the stages in which the sociological perspective has gradually broadened out to include the kinds of processes discussed in this chapter.

# 5

# Sociological interpretations of juvenile delinquency

This chapter tries to draw out from the enormous amount of material on juvenile delinquency generated by sociologists some of the main developments in sociological interpretations of the phenomenon. There are two particular dangers in this approach. The first danger is that of imposing a spurious continuity on these interpretations by implying that each was a logical modification of a preceding interpretation; in fact, some of these investigations and interpretations grew out of very different ongoing sociological traditions and might be said to contradict rather than complement or logically modify each other. Thus, while the approach adopted here is broadly a historical one which traces the major changes in conceptualizations of the phenomenon, in fact it should be remembered that there is not a consensus among sociologists about the 'right' perspective to adopt; as a result many sociologists may partially subscribe to each of the following general orientations. The second danger is that in selecting and abstracting out only one or two ideas from each main 'school' or author, the richness of the particular contribution is lost and, at the same time, what was said may be distorted by pulling it out of context; the only solution to this is for the reader to examine the original contributions for himself.

The selection from and criticism of particular works here are inevitably highly particular and done broadly from the standpoint of the deviance perspective presented earlier; thus all that can be provided is a general orientation to the sociological tradition of delinquency explanation.

The special meaning of the term 'juvenile delinquency' must first be clarified. The word 'delinquency' is typically used to refer to juvenile acts which would be crimes if done by adults; it also includes a range of 'status' offences or acts which can only be committed by juveniles by definition (e.g., drinking under age, truancy, driving under age). Various 'welfare' cases in which technically no criminal law may have been broken but where the child may be considered beyond control of the parents or in need of care and protection are typically also included in the category of delinquency. 'Delinquency', then, is a more inclusive category than that of 'crime', although the range of inclusion varies considerably between societies.

The introduction of a special word to categorize certain juvenile acts has both legal and social policy implications, for the official intention of the label 'delinquent' is to suggest that a given act is something less than a crime when committed by a juvenile; industrial societies have thus developed official processes for dealing with officially identified delinquents which are partially separated from the adult processing procedures. In fact, there is no agreement between societies on the age range of juvenile delinquency, and within societies such definitions change over time; in England and Wales the age of criminal responsibility was raised from eight to ten in 1965 and was raised again to fourteen in 1969. Thus the proceedings for dealing with children below fourteen will be civil and not criminal when the 1969 Act is implemented; for those between fourteen and the seventeenth birthday, the separate juvenile

court system is preserved and they are still officially delinquents; finally, those between 17 and 21, whilst dealt with
by adult courts, are referred to as 'young offenders' in an
attempt to retain a tenuous distinction between them and
adult offenders, and there are some special court sentences
available for this group. The terms 'juvenile delinquency'
and 'juvenile delinquent' are thus legal categories whose
actual meaning and content vary considerably between
societies, juveniles of the same ages and offences being dealt
with in different ways in different societies; this makes
meaningful cross-cultural comparisons of patterns of delinquency difficult. Also, if, as has been suggested, the character of the social control processes contribute to the form
and size of the phenomenon, then the relevance of theories
generated in one society to the understanding of the phenomenon in others where control processes may be very different must be questioned.

Before looking at some of the main contributions to the
sociological tradition, a preliminary issue must be raised
briefly: why has such a large proportion of the work of
those sociologists who have specialized in the study of
crime been concerned with the study of the juvenile? The
answers reflect both the particular social and political
concerns of industrial societies and also the particular
personal values and interests of the investigating sociologists. There has been a marked change in these societies'
attitudes towards children and the role of the state in
relation to them since the middle of the nineteenth century.
In the specific case of law-breaking the change has been
from simple punishment and equality before the law with
adults to a recognition of children's welfare needs and the
state's responsibility to meet these. Officially then, punishment of law-breaking children is supposed to be moderated
by a consideration of individual welfare. In effect, being

a juvenile in the eyes of the law is an extra mitigating circumstance to be taken into account in the disposition of the case. A further reason is the belief that subsequent criminality stems from early involvement in delinquency, so that if prevention of future criminality is a concern, then the 'root' of the problem, juvenile delinquency, should be investigated; certainly a proportion, about half in most studies, of official adult offenders have also been officially identified as juveniles, but we have little knowledge of the nature of the career transition from official juvenile to official adult offender. In fact it is the official statistics themselves which provide the main clue to this major social and sociological preoccupation with the juvenile offender, for these show that officially the peak age for indictable offences in England and Wales was fourteen for a long period (between the raising of the school-leaving age from fourteen to fifteen, just after the war, to the recent re-classification of a group of non-indictable offences popular among adolescents as indictable); thus the early teens provide the period of greatest official risk. However, Power (1962) has shown that if non-indictable offences (many of which are equally as 'serious' as the indictable offences committed by juveniles) are added to the indictable, then the official peak age is more likely to be about 18 or 19. Thus, even society's reliance on the official statistics is found to be somewhat misguided when the full range of offences are taken into account. Nevertheless, late childhood and adolescence are seen to be the years of greatest risk of being caught for law-breaking, and this has resulted in considerable pressure on criminologists and sociologists to investigate this as a distinct problem.

Finally, in terms of the sociologist's own concerns and apart from any political pressure he may experience or personal interest he may have in the issue of delinquency, at the practical level of research the juvenile delinquent is likely to be defined as a much easier subject to study than his adult counterpart; the juvenile is more visible, accessible, gullible, less able to say no and subject to wider official control than the adult. Moreover, his law-breaking is typically more mundane and trivial so that the consequences of his confiding in an outsider, such as a sociologist, are likely to be defined by him as less serious than would be the case with the adult offender. Of course, none of this necessarily means that the data which sociologists obtain from juveniles are any more (or less) reliable than those obtained from adults; that is something which can be decided not in the abstract but only in the investigation of the methodology of each study. Convenience is therefore an added reason for sociologists' concentration on juvenile offenders.

With the exception of the last point, and then only in part, the reasons given for sociologists' extensive concentration on juvenile offenders stem not from sociological values or problems but from the definition of juvenile delinquency as a social and political problem. Through political processes particular groups in society can influence heavily what sociologists study; this brings us back to the points made in the first chapter concerning the value problems of traditional criminology. Exactly the same problem has dogged much sociological investigation of crime and delinquency and has resulted frequently in a blinkered approach to the selection of issues and processes for study. The metaphorical blinkers worn by many sociologists in their investigation of delinquency were a result, to a considerable extent, of the fact that the sociologists themselves took-for-granted and shared the society's definition of the problem; thus many of their explanations seemed to be offered up in response to such political concerns as the 'causes' of delinquency and means of eradicating these, and ways of changing those officially found guilty. Few sociologists, until recently, recognized that their asking and trying to answer these questions were simply tying them to the political status quo and obscuring the investigation of more fundamental issues which are posed in the deviance perspective.

It was noted in the last chapter that the main official parameters of crime derived from the official statistics focus attention on young working-class males who, usually in small groups, indulge in a wide range of property offences, minor forms of violence and, more recently, offences connected with the motor car; basically it is this combination of parameters for which sociologists have offered a variety of interpretations, the main themes of which are now considered.

Most sociological interpretations of delinquency and crime lack a sense of history; those that attempt to account for the origins and emergence of typical patterns of delinquency, for example some sub-cultural explanations, rarely attempt to locate such origins in time and place. Similarly, those explanations focusing on the processes of transmission of delinquent values, such as Sutherland's theory of differential association (Sutherland and Cressey, 1960), claim to be concerned with processes that are universally present irrespective of time and place so that history is not a direct concern. Thus the kinds of explanations proposed by sociologists tend to be either classificatory or processual. The classificatory approaches usually provide a set of concepts which are used to classify the actual content and forms of delinquent behaviour; such classification schemes are not equipped to deal with historical processes and only rarely is the historical dimension of the emergence and changes in form and content of delinquency dealt with by sociologists in their discussions accompanying their classification schemes. The most obvious example of such a scheme would be Merton's paradigm for understanding the relationships between patterns of deviant behaviour and certain features of the social structure (Merton, 1963); this will be discussed shortly. In fact, this kind of classification scheme attempts to account for contemporary patterns of delinquency by looking at the contemporary social structure. On the other hand, the processual approaches, like differential association, would claim that history is not important for them because their concern is not with particular behaviours but with general processes which are present irrespective of the particular form they may take. Contemporary rather than historical examples are used to illustrate these universal processes for obvious methodological reasons.

This ahistorical character of sociological interpretations of delinquency is a serious shortcoming because these interpretations invariably rest on taken-for-granted assumptions concerning the history of particular societies or communities. A feature common to most interpretations is their attempt to relate particular patterns of individual or group delinquencies to aspects of the social structure; the sociologist has generally tried to show how the overall social position of groups, measured in terms of such things as social class, social status or educational attainments, provides the background conditions for the emergence and persistence of shared values among those sharing similar social structural positions. In the study of delinquency, this typically meant focusing on the community or neighbourhood in which official delinquents were most frequently found and examining selected aspects of neighbourhood life considered relevant to the understanding of delinquency; the communities typically studied were those occupying

122

the inner areas of large cities, for it is these in which the highest official crime rates most frequently occur. Explanations offered for patterns of delinquency in such areas, with a few exceptions, fail to account for or often to even consider the sheer historical continuity and persistency of the official patterns. A major problem facing sociological interpretation of delinquency is the fact that many of the areas which are contemporarily officially defined as high delinquency areas were high delinquency areas more than a hundred years ago and have consistently maintained their official rates throughout the past century.

Data from several sources clearly illustrates this continuity; Tobias (1967) provides a valuable analysis of the official patterns of crime in England in the nineteenth century using both official statistics and a wide array of documentary sources from the period. The so-called 'criminal class' grew out of and was largely maintained by the recruitment of often vagrant but skilled juveniles who were trained and frequently kept by adults for their thieving capacities. As is clear from Mayhew's vivid descriptions, the 'rookeries' in which such juveniles and criminals abounded were often those areas which continued to have high official delinquency rates a hundred or so years later. Mayhew (1862), himself no mean classificatory criminologist, distinguished three main types of young felons who emerged from the mass of younger juvenile thieves: common thieves, expert pickpockets and burglars. One might add to Mayhew's actual observations the fictionalized account of Morrison (1896) in *A Child of the Jago*, written more than forty years after Mayhew's work. The Jago, 'for one hundred years the blackest pit in London', was a notorious web of streets which, although long demolished and replaced by different streets and housing, nevertheless, has maintained consistently high official delinquency rates since the time of Morrison's writing. This problem of historical continuity will be considered subsequently in relation to specific theories.

In looking at the historical roots of the sociological interpretation of delinquency, there were several other nineteenth century writers and researchers, apart from Mayhew, whose work provides a background against which to set more recent contributions. The statistical analyses of the continental writers Guerry and Quetelet were the first attempts to relate the official crime statistics to a range of population and geographical indices. At about the same time as Mayhew in England, a German, Avé-Lallement, although not specifically concerned with juvenile delinquency proposed a sophisticated thesis to account for the growth and persistence of criminal groups with their own argot and traditions; he saw such groups gradually emerging from the widespread vagrancy which followed the break-up of the old feudal order. He argued that these vagrant groups, which lived by petty crime and from the proceeds of almsgiving, were forced to change their habits with the rapid growth of cities in the eighteenth and nineteenth centuries, and the concomitant development of organized police systems. They were increasingly pushed back into the social order by these new social controllers and were forced to operate by stealth in the relative anonymity of the new cities (Lindesmith and Levin, 1937). Mayhew also had suggested the importance of the urban vagrants as a major source of recruitment to the 'criminal class' of the nineteenth century. Here, then, was perhaps the first attempt to account for patterns of crime as a direct product of features of the social structure; it is this kind of general all-embracing theory of crime which is echoed in several more recent contributions.

For many years following these early contributions, the

124

main interest of those investigators of a sociological in-
clination was in the relationship between crime and delinquency and economic conditions, the general standpoint
of such authors being the thesis that poverty was a main
'cause' of criminality. These studies, based almost entirely
on the analysis of official criminal statistics and their relationship to a series of socio-economic indices, were incon-
clusive and often contradictory. Vold (1958) provides a
useful summary of their findings and some of the difficulties
of interpreting them.

However, it was not until the 1920s and '30s that any
significant developments occurred in the study of delinquency. Then they grew out of a small-scale revolution
in sociological ideas and methods which took place at the
University of Chicago. The city of Chicago was viewed as
a natural laboratory for sociological research by the outstanding sociologists who worked there, and a remarkable
series of studies was carried through into a wide range
of subjects. Whilst the subjects chosen for study often
reflected the major social and political concerns of the
period, especially those arising out of city life and the
successive waves of immigration experienced in America,
they also reflected the natural personal and increasingly
sociological curiosity of the particular investigators with
the less respectable aspects of city life. The main instigator
of this upsurge of research activity was Robert Park; at
the same time George Herbert Mead (1934), also at Chicago,
was laying the theoretical foundations of one of the main
traditions in sociology, symbolic interactionism. Crime and
in particular juvenile delinquency were interests of several
Chicago sociologists; these interests were reflected in a two-
pronged approach to the investigation and explanation of
delinquency in Chicago.

The first style of investigation was an attempt to apply

the social ecological theories of Park (1925) to the study of delinquency. Drawing on ecological ideas from biology and zoology which emphasized the mutual interdependence of plant and animal species in a given area, their conflicting but coordinated interests and the processes of competition, dominance and succession among different species, Park analysed the social organization of the city using the same concepts. The latter was seen as comprising a series of natural social areas which emerged during the processes of city growth and economic development and were particularly contingent on the process of competition for control of the city's natural resources. Park saw the modern city as comprising five main natural areas which formed a series of concentric zones around the city centre; each zone had distinctive social and physical characteristics. An important feature of the social ecological approach was to view the social relationships and typical behaviours persisting among those who inhabited each zone as natural social relationships and responses which emerged out of the environmental conditions of the zone. These ideas were originally applied to the phenomenon of delinquency by Shaw and McKay (1942), first in Chicago and subsequently in a large number of other American cities. Relating official statistics on delinquency to census population data, Shaw and McKay computed official delinquency rates by census tract for the whole of the city over a period of almost thirty years. They found gross and consistent differences in the rates between the five zones defined by Park; the rates declined proportionately with distance from the city centre, and the highest rates were mostly found in the 'interstitial' zone which surrounded the city centre. This zone, the city's 'twilight' area, was characterized by high population mobility, poor housing, and overcrowding and was increasingly corroded by industry; in its social class composition it was almost completely working class. This pattern of delinquency distribution was more or less reproduced in later ecological studies of other cities. In line with Park's thesis, these high delinquency areas were viewed as natural areas, the delinquency of the boys being seen as largely a normal response to the social and natural characteristics of these communities.

In spite of the natural and normal character of most delinquency when seen as a response to environmental characteristics, the main orienting concept used by sociologists of the Chicago School to understand social and urban problems like delinquency was that of 'social disorganization'; the ecologists and others tended to view the emergence of high delinquency rates in a community as one indicator of the social disorganization of that community. Louis Wirth (1964) and W. I. Thomas (1966) were two of the Chicago sociologists who used this concept to account for a range of social problems, and Burgess (1942), a collaborator of Park's, later went on to apply the concept to Shaw and McKay's findings. Thomas defined social disorganization as 'a decrease of the influence of existing social rules of behaviour upon individual members of the group'.

Now, as C. Wright Mills (1963a) pointed out many years ago, this concept has unfortunate implications which render its value in sociological analysis questionable. There are two main problems in using it, one a value problem and the other an empirical problem. Firstly, if a social situation is defined by the observer as disorganized, it can only be disorganized in relation to a given set of principles of organization; but what happened all too frequently when this term was used was that the principles of organization were assumed or taken-for-granted and were not spelled out by the observer; invariably it turned out that the

127

principles of organization used as a yardstick for disorganization were the observer's own implicit, usually
conventionally middle-class, values concerning what *ought*
to be. Thus his own values entered directly into his diagnosis of social disorganization. Secondly, if a situation is
defined as disorganized, this denies the presence of any
typical features of organized relationships. Empirically this
is untenable, for the very behaviours taken as indicators
of disorganization actually require a high degree of social
organization; delinquency and crime are social activities
requiring cooperation, trust and persistence of relationships
if they are to be even minimally successful. The concept
of social disorganization, used to diagnose social problems,
therefore misleads because it draws attention away from
the very features of social relationships through which
delinquency and other such phenomena persist. The
Chicago sociologists were unable to see the implications
of the concept; organization was certainly present in high
delinquency areas, but it was not of the form which fitted
in with their conceptions of 'appropriate' organization.

One possible use of the concept of social disorganization
which seems less open to the above criticisms is in cross-
cultural comparisons. It may be possible to distinguish different levels of social disorganization between societies;
thus societies in states of civil war, where there may be
several warring factions or where there is a dissensus about
the appropriate form of central government, may be disorganized relative both to their history and to other societies
with similar economic and social structures but without
such conflicts. Clearly within such a 'disorganized' society
the various factions and interest groups could be highly
organized; obvious contemporary examples would be Viet-
nam and Cambodia. Thus between societies it may be possible to distinguish levels of disorganization according to

indices of major internal conflict and instability of previously institutionalized relationships. Such a comparison
does not deny the presence of highly organized groups
within such a society and takes as its norm of organization
either other similar societies or the same society in an
earlier period rather than the investigator's implicit personal values. This use of the term comes close in meaning
to the concept of anomie, which will be briefly discussed
later.

The main contribution of the ecological branch of the
Chicago school was thus to emphasize the normality of
delinquency in certain neighbourhoods and to point to the
importance of local community characteristics as providing
a natural setting in which delinquent values emerged and
persisted. Shaw and McKay had also established that over
80 per cent of the official delinquents committed their
delinquencies in the company of a few other boys of about
the same age; delinquency was very much a group enterprise. It was the study of these delinquent peer groups and
gangs which formed the second major contribution of the
Chicago school to the analysis of delinquency. Two works
in particular are outstanding in their contribution both
to the substantive field of delinquency research and to the
methodological tradition of general sociology; these are *The
Gang* by F. M. Thrasher (1927) and *Street Corner Society*
by W. F. Whyte (1963).

These two studies complement both each other, being
substantively very different, and also, when taken together,
the work of Shaw and McKay. Thrasher, in his mammoth
study of over 1,300 boys' gangs in Chicago during the 1920s,
traced the typical careers of these groups, showing how
the spontaneous play groups of early childhood developed
into the highly structured adolescent gangs with their own
traditions, argot, sense of loyalty and control of a 'terri-

tory'. Conflict was a central concern of the typical gang, and of particular interest in terms of the deviance perspective was Thrasher's suggestion that gangs increasingly cohered around the values of conflict and aggression as a response to the various attempts by adults and other adolescent groups to forcibly control their activities. Thrasher argued that gangs which indulged intermittently in delinquencies flourished both because they met the common individual needs of belonging and protection and also because the environment facilitated delinquency in a variety of ways, such as the collusion of adults in delinquent activities and weak family controls.

Whyte's study was of a very different kind than that of Thrasher, being an account of one particular group of young men, the Norton Street Gang, whose company Whyte shared for three years. Although not specifically concerned with delinquency and crime and although the members of the group were young men rather than juveniles, several of Whyte's findings pointed to aspects of the dynamics of group life which are held to be relevant to an understanding of delinquent peer groups and which have been followed up by subsequent delinquency researchers. Firstly, at a general level, Whyte's study of this group and its position in the local social structure is an explicit refutation of the social disorganization approach. Two other features of his study are important: his distinction between 'corner boys' and 'college boys' posed a problem for subsequent research which has yet to be resolved satisfactorily. He found that in this socio-economically homogenous slum two distinct responses emerged among adolescents. A minority attempted to achieve social mobility by a conscious commitment to middle-class or college values, with the eventual hope of moving out of 'Cornerville'. There was an early and almost complete split between them and the 'corner boys'.

Two distinctive styles of life emerged among adolescents which were mutually exclusive; it was impossible to be a 'college boy' and still run with the 'corner boys'. In Whyte's own words:

> Both the college boy and the corner boy want to get ahead. The difference between them is that the college boy either does not tie himself to a group of close friends or else is willing to sacrifice his friendship with those who do not advance as fast as he does. The corner boy is tied to his group by a network of reciprocal obligations from which he is either unwilling or unable to break away. (Whyte, 1966, p. 107)

The roots of this differential response to the slum situation have yet to be clarified by sociologists. Finally, Whyte's analysis of the intra-group relationships, and especially his emphasis on the importance of the leader in influencing and controlling the group's activities, pointed to areas of analysis which were picked up and elaborated by later sub-cultural theorists. Whyte's study is the classic piece of participant observational research in sociology.

The theory of differential association proposed by E. H. Sutherland and intended as an all-embracing explanation of the process of learning to become a criminal can be seen as an attempt to marry the two levels of analysis found in the Chicago school's studies (Sutherland and Cressey, 1960). Sutherland hypothesized that a person becomes a criminal or a delinquent when he experiences an excess of definitions encouraging law violation over definitions encouraging law-abiding behaviour; these definitions are mediated to the individual largely within intimate personal groups such as the peer group or the family. Sutherland's use of the term 'definitions' is really a shorthand version of the concept 'definition of the situation' and is derived from the writing of W. I. Thomas (1966); in the context of the theory of differential association, Sutherland was referring to the extent both of one's association with others whose definitions of some situations encouraged the breaking of particular laws and also of one's isolation from others whose definitions of the same situations discouraged the breaking of these laws. The associations an individual has with pro-criminal values and behaviour, that is, the nature of his exposure to them, can vary in frequency, duration, priority and intensity.

Unfortunately the theory, as it stands is untestable, for it requires some sort of total accounting method in which an individual's life experiences of definitions favourable and unfavourable to law violation are balanced against each other; the impossibility of devising such a method in social research will be clear. Nevertheless, Sutherland's theory, despite being empirically problematic, did serve to direct sociologists' attention to the processes of interaction within face-to-face groups; these processes were present in both those neighbourhoods with high and those with low delinquency rates. It would follow from Sutherland's thesis that the association of juveniles with pro-criminal and anti-criminal values would be very different in the two neighbourhoods; this differential association comprised the process of becoming delinquent for Sutherland. It seemed to be this theory, taken in conjunction with Merton's discussion of anomie which provided the impetus for the emergence of the sub-cultural approach to the explanation of delinquency during the 1950s.

Merton's essay was an attempt to clarify and extend the meaning of 'anomie', a term introduced into sociology by Durkheim. Durkheim (1951, 1965) had used the term to describe extreme situations of normlessness, that is, situations where no clear-cut guides for behaviour existed and where previous solutions to everyday problems of living were rendered inappropriate by sudden changes in the social structure; examples of the kind of situation envisaged by Durkheim would be a sudden drastic economic crisis or an unexpected invasion by a foreign power. In situations such as these, the firmly held values and expectations of many sections of the population are called dramatically into question and are rendered irrelevant to the problems faced. Merton's use of the term, however, differs sharply from that of Durkheim (Merton, 1963).

A main concern of Merton was to account for the differential societal distribution of rates of various kinds of deviant behaviour. He argued that societies can be analysed in terms of, firstly, the dominant goals which all members are encouraged to seek, and secondly, the legitimate or socially approved ways of achieving these goals; when there is what he called an 'acute disjunction' between the goals and the means for large sections of the population, this results in strong pressures to deviate from the approved norms. It was this disjunction which he defined as 'anomie'. The prime example he took was contemporary American society, in which, he argued, the dominant goal to which all are encouraged to strive is material success through occupational mobility; however, such success is only available through legitimate occupational channels for a minority of the population. Those most unlikely to succeed are the bottom echelons of the social class hierarchy, and it is among such groups that the acute disjunction or anomie is likely to be experienced most vividly; the pressure to deviate is therefore at its strongest among the most economically and socially disadvantaged groups. As a result, many decide to deviate from legitimate norms in order to achieve the material rewards, and they develop their own means for achieving the goals. He calls this the response of 'innovation' to the situation of anomie. There are other adaptations to these pressures, and he calls these variously: 'conformity', 'retreatism', 'ritualism' and 'rebellion'. However, the important response in the present context is that of innovation, for the characteristic innovation, he argues, is property theft; he thus accounts for the high official rates for property offences among lower working-class groups as an adaptation to the structural strain induced by the disjunction between the goal of material success and the lack of legitimate means for its achievement.

It is unnecessary here to provide an extensive critique of Merton's theory, for this has been done by several authors (see Clinard, 1964), notably Lemert; however, in terms of the deviance perspective, it is worth noting the following points. The theory accepts the official rates of deviance as actually reflecting the real phenomenon to be explained; the distinction between goals and means is tenuous and artificial; the assumption that everybody shares the same basic goal is a simplification and distortion of the complexities involved in analysing people's life goals; no account is taken of the problematic processes of social control; the model is static and suggests no hypotheses about interaction, for example, in relation to the movement into and out of deviant careers; within the situation of acute disjunction it does not account for differential responses to strain, that is, why in a situation of anomie some conform, some innovate, some retreat and so on; finally, by focusing on the structural level, it plays down the importance of typical social meanings as they enter into individuals' interpretations of their situations by implying that these meanings are merely products of external social forces. Merton's model, nevertheless, when taken in conjunction with the earlier work on delinquency and peer group processes of Shaw and McKay, Thrasher, Whyte,

Sutherland and others, provided the basis for the sub-cultural approach to understanding delinquency.

The concept of sub-culture is an attempt to deal analytically with the apparent fact that a range of small 'societies', characterized by some values that seemingly conflict with or differ from those of conventional society, are contained within the political unit of the total society; industrial societies are differentiated into a variety of strata or groups each possessing some distinctive values and behaviour patterns. It is these 'societies' contained within the larger one which are referred to generally as 'sub-cultures'. The central problem in the use of the term for understanding the social action of any particular group is: where does the general culture end and sub-culture begin? Are there values which are common to all members of a culture? If so, what are they and how can one differentiate them from the values which are said to be peculiar to particular sub-cultures?

There have been two useful attempts to relate the discussion of specifically delinquent or criminal sub-cultures to the more general use of the term in sociology by Downes (1966) in his review of delinquent sub-cultural theory and by Wolfgang and Ferracuti (1967) in their essay on violent sub-cultures. Both these discussions lie within the traditional sociological framework; they therefore largely ignore the kinds of issues and criticisms just levelled at Merton's anomie theory and which are also largely applicable to sub-culture theory. However, their discussions do illustrate clearly the difficulties of using the term 'sub-culture' even when it is used within a traditional framework. Both show that except in a very few cases it is difficult analytically to distinguish sub-cultural from general values and that in traditional methodology we have few reliable techniques for measuring values even when we can distinguish them.

135

Both seem to agree that the concept can be used most usefully in relation to those groups some of whose activities run directly counter to values assumed to characterize clearly the general or politically potent culture. The responses of these groups to some of the situations which they face are described by Downes as negative responses to the social and cultural structures and can be seen in the actions of delinquent or politically extremist groups; in similar terms, Wolfgang and Ferracuti see the actions of such groups as reflecting intolerated discordant values. Unfortunately, when the difficulties of using the concept, which are raised by Downes and Wolfgang and Ferracuti, are taken together with those criticisms which arise from the deviance perspective, already outlined in relation to the anomie theory, then the concept seems to have serious shortcomings if it is used on its own as a main explanatory device. Some of these shortcomings are illustrated in the main contributions to delinquent sub-culture theory. The disagreement between the writers is one basic problem of the utility of the concept.

The first of a series of attempts to understand gang delinquency in sub-cultural terms was that of Cohen (1955) in his book *Delinquent Boys*. Starting from Merton's anomie scheme he argued that the innovation adaptation failed to account for the distinctive content of the delinquency of working-class boys' gangs. Far from being an attempt to achieve material success through rationally calculated property theft, much delinquency was non-utilitarian and negativistic in character; a great deal of juvenile theft was not done to, and could not, provide the thieves with an illicit income. Nor could the vandalism, damage to property, conflict activities and fleeting escapades with motor cars be construed as attempts to achieve material success by illegitimate means. In fact, Cohen argues, these delinquent activities frequently seemed to be a direct denial of the essentially middle-class values of getting ahead by hard work and material acquisition. This led him to propose a theory of 'reaction formation'. He hypothesized that working-class boys, like others, share a common problem of status, of gaining recognition and acceptance in the community; however, the boys are ill-prepared by their home and social environment to perform effectively in terms of the conventional criteria of status. These criteria, mediated largely by the school and by other representatives of the politically dominant culture, consist of things like academic achievement and ambition, good manners, ability to postpone gratification, respect for property, ability to control aggression and constructive use of leisure; they comprise the 'middle-class measuring rod' by which the boys' performances are measured and rewarded. Because many working-class boys perform inadequately in terms of these criteria, as is constantly made clear to them in school, they are forced to create their own criteria for status and reward; Cohen argues that the boys set up their own criteria by turning upside down the middle-class measuring rod and giving status for those activities which are the very antithesis of its components. Many of their own criteria lead directly to delinquent activities. It is this turning upside down of middle-class values, to recoup some of the esteem denied to them by the conventional culture, which is the core of Cohen's explanation for the emergence of the distinctive content of juvenile delinquency and therefore of the delinquent sub-culture.

Two other contributors to the sub-cultural tradition provide contrasting accounts of the delinquent sub-culture. Cloward and Ohlin (1960), in proposing a typology of subcultures to account for distinct styles of delinquency which they claim characterize different neighbourhoods, directly modify Merton's theory. They argue that Merton only talked about the availability of legitimate means for achieving material success and ignored illegitimate means. They argue that all youths internalize middle-class success goals at an early age, but in most working-class neighbourhoods legitimate avenues for mobility and success are largely closed; however, there may be clear channels for mobility in organized criminal rackets and professional crime. Where these illegitimate means for success are present, the type of delinquency they suggest is very different from that in neighbourhoods where adult criminality is unorganized and small-scale. In the first, delinquency tends to reflect and be continuous with adult criminality, being rationally organized for material gain; in the second, delinquency tends to be characterized by the concerns of adolescence in a loosely controlled environment centering particularly on aggression of various kinds against other people and property. Finally, there is a third sub-culture comprising the 'double-failures' and drop-outs who, in response to their failure both in legitimate and illegitimate enterprises, take to various kinds of escapist activity, especially hard drug use. These three juvenile sub-cultures – criminal, conflict and retreatist – thus arise as a response to the particular pressures and opportunities of their immediate environment.

A third contribution is that of Miller (1958). Working in an anthropological rather than a sociological tradition. Miller emphasizes different aspects of the delinquent sub-culture in his analysis. He sees a clear split between middle-class culture and the culture of the group at the bottom of the American working class; the two cultures are viewed as quite autonomous, with their own traditions and life-styles. There is little room for overlap or penetration of one culture by the other in Miller's explanation. The culture of the lower working-class is characterized by six 'focal concerns': trouble, toughness, smartness, excitement, fate and autonomy. These concerns are issues which constantly require the attention of the members of the culture in a variety of common situations, and attachment to the concerns can lead to delinquency in various ways. The origins of these concerns are related to the gradual bedding down of the American class structure following the successive waves of immigration; the bottom section consists of Negroes and the hard core of families of unsuccessful immigrants. Miller argues that the distinctive family structure and relationships which characterize this bottom stratum, especially the female-based household and single-sex peer groups, contribute to and reinforce the delinquency producing aspects of the focal concerns. He thus sees the total social structure comprising at least two distinctive class styles which are culturally discontinuous, one of which generates delinquency as part of its very nature.

There are other contributions to the tradition of delinquent sub-cultural theory (e.g., Yablonsky, 1967), but these suffice to illustrate the variety of interpretations offered to account for the distinctive patterns of American delinquency. Apart from the criticisms already applied to the anomie theory and which can also be applied to most of the sub-cultural approaches, the fact that the theories of Cohen, Cloward and Ohlin, and Miller offer very different and sometimes conflicting explanations for the same phenomena is in itself a major problem of the sub-culture approach. These theories were based on each author's personal observations, which were inevitably limited in scope; unfortunately, they were usually presented as definitive and universally applicable formulations, whereas the nature of their origins suggests that they should be treated as tentative hypotheses. None of them are characterized by a methodology which could be compared to the careful, empirical work of Thrasher and Whyte.

Nevertheless they did give rise to a series of empirical studies in America which have tried to investigate, among other things, whether these theories were supported when subjected to more rigorous research study. The work of Gold (1963), who was concerned in part with Cohen's thesis, Spergel (1964), who investigated the Cloward and Ohlin typology, and Short and Strodtbeck (1965), whose study is relevant to all the theories mentioned, best illustrate through research practice the empirical difficulties of the concept of the sub-culture. At the empirical level these studies, and in particular the work of Short and Strodtbeck, suggest that the clear-cut, neat explanations of the sub-cultural theorists do not adequately represent the complex processes leading to group delinquency. A main problem has been their almost exclusive concern with the structured gang; the available evidence, both American and English, suggests that the mass of delinquent acts are not committed by organized delinquent gangs but by small, fairly transient and loosely structured friendship groups; the role of the gang has thus been overemphasized in these theories. Similarly, only a tenuous commitment was found to specifically delinquent values, and those values which were espoused fairly consistently by official delinquents (for example, sexual prowess, being 'cool' or 'sharp') were not so much opposed to middle-class values, as Cohen suggested, but were rather alternatives to them. This empirical evidence fits in well with the most trenchant theoretical critique of the sub-cultural tradition, that of Matza (1964) in *Delinquency and Drift*. It is Matza's critique which provides the link between the mainstream of delinquency theory, found in the notion of sub-culture, and those writing from within the expanding deviance perspective.

Matza argues that the sub-cultural theories suffered from one of the same faults as traditional criminology by presenting a highly deterministic view of the sub-cultural delinquent; each of the above, and other theories, implies that the childhood and adolescent male peer groups who commit a range of delinquencies are organized around the central value of delinquency and that the group members are fully committed to this value. The group and its main values and interests are pictured as being largely cut off and distinct from the ongoing conventional culture. Matza, in his own investigations, which are supported by Short and Strodtbeck's subsequent work, found that, far from this being the case, there was a distinct lack of commitment to specifically delinquent values. In fact, boys were often very ambivalent about their own delinquent activities and experienced guilt in relation to them; guilt would certainly not be present if the boys were fully committed to their delinquencies. Matza argues that the values which characterize delinquency, namely the search for excitement, a distaste for mundane hard work, and masculinity, are not specific to the delinquent sub-culture nor are they the antithesis of middle-class values; he suggests that, on the contrary, these values are distributed throughout the various social classes, but they emerge on different occasions and in different situations for different social groups. In the middle class, for example, these values typically emerge in the leisure situation, in sports or other ritual events. He calls this sharing of values 'subterranean convergence'; these values, perhaps less respectable in the middle class, are kept below the surface for most of the time and only emerge in certain specially designated situations.

However, not only do the working-class boys' mundane delinquencies reflect badly timed extensions of commonly held values, but the delinquent can only be understood by recognizing that he is completely surrounded and dealt with by conventional culture and its various agents of social control. The delinquent sub-culture cannot therefore be viewed as cut-off, outside or separate from the main body of society as earlier theorists had implied. Matza goes on to develop a thesis in which the mundane delinquent is seen in a situation of drift, committed neither to a conventional nor a deviant value system but flirting first with one, then with the other; the situation of drift is exacerbated by recurring features of the lower-working-class boy's social situation, especially by the long periods of boredom at school, home and work, and by the extensive but empty periods of leisure. These often give rise to a mood of fatalism or desperation which facilitates the drift into delinquency.

Finally, Matza describes a series of common 'techniques of neutralization' which the boys use to justify their delinquencies to themselves in particular circumstances while knowing them to be wrong; to free himself from the moral bind of the law which he recognizes most of the time, the boy uses special justifications or neutralizations which make the act right for him in that situation on that particular occasion. Calling these neutralizations of the bind of law into play allows him to commit the act with a relative lack of guilt feelings at the time. Without listing these techniques, it is sufficient to note that Matza goes back to the law itself to locate the neutralizations, for he argues that the delinquents' justifications are but extensions of common, legitimate legal defences; these defences would normally lead to findings of innocence or at least to a lessening of the legal penalty by demonstrating that mitigating circumstances were present at the commission of the crime.

Matza thus attempts to escape from the determinism of sub-culture theory by proposing a theory of drift which draws attention to the total surrounding and penetrating of the working-class boy's culture by conventional culture and especially by agents of and beliefs about the legal system. From the deviance perspective the four important features of his contribution are, firstly, its critique of sociological positivism or determinism; secondly, his stress on the similarity of and interaction between the culture of delinquency and the conventional culture; thirdly, the introduction of aspects of social control agencies and especially the legal system as sources of the delinquents' justifications for their delinquencies; and finally, the role which he gives to the meanings which the delinquents themselves attach to their acts as providing the ultimate means to sociological understanding.

The empirical and theoretical shortcomings of the sub-cultural approach were increasingly realized as a result of some of the research undertaken in relation to delinquency, through Matza's critique and through the growing interest in the work of those writing from within the deviance p spective who drew attention to fundamental proble, touched by the proponents of sub-culture. An early indication of this can be found in a study by Piliavin and Briar (1964) of police encounters with juveniles. Noting the immense latitude given to police officers in their decisions to formally arrest and charge juveniles or to deal with them less formally, they studied the features of the situation of encounter between police and juvenile suspects which influenced police officers' decisions on how to handle the cases. They concluded that the police had clear pictures or stereotypes of what they conceived to be basically 'good' boys and serious troublemakers; they tended to base their official dispositions of the cases very much on these personal 'theories' of what the 'real' delinquent was like. The thing that influenced these stereotypes most strongly was the youths' demeanour, that is, how they dressed and especially how they behaved towards the officers, the uncooperative, aggressive youths being seen as the potential serious troublemakers and as the 'real' delinquents. A later study by Skolnick (1966), concerned not specifically with juvenile delinquency but with the general social organization of the police and their processes of law enforcement, considers in much greater detail some of the issues raised by Piliavin and Briar and others by analysing the relationships between the police and the community in one city.

The move away from the sub-cultural approach has been influenced and reinforced by the work of Cicourel. Heavily influenced himself by the social phenomenology of A. Schuetz, who saw the central task in sociology as the study of subjective meaning structures, Cicourel's own work reflects a continuing concern with the relationship between theory and research in sociology. Apart from his main work on methodology (Cicourel, 1964), several of his most important contributions to sociology have been in the area of crime and delinquency. His influential early paper, written with Kitsuse, redefines the sociological uses of the official statistics; it was they who first proposed the argument discussed in the previous chapter, that official statistics must be viewed as indices of official organizational activities and that one sociological task is to elucidate the meanings and activities through which the statistics were organizationally produced (Cicourel and Kitsuse, 1963a). The work of Piliavin and Briar is an example of a study which clarifies the processes of official record compilation by the police. In a further piece of research, again in collaboration with Kitsuse, Cicourel investigates the processes of decision-making in the school (Cicourel and Kitsuse, 1963b). Like the organizations in the penal system, the school can be seen as an organization producing various 'official' rates such as a college-going rate, a truancy rate or an early drop-out rate; these and other rates reflect and are composed of different kinds of adolescent careers within the school such as the 'high achiever', the 'persistent truant' and the 'unstable under-achiever'. The interest of Cicourel and Kitsuse is in how labels such as the above come to be attached to children in school and in the effects of the teachers' use of these labels on both the children and the various organizational rates. This kind of study, in seeing the school as an organization in which delinquent careers can emerge and which produces, among other rates, a delinquency rate, has obvious relevance to the study of delinquency.

Cicourel's most recent study of how official files and statistics on juvenile delinquency are assembled in two cities is an extended investigation of his previous concerns (Cicourel, 1968). Comparing the two cities, Cicourel shows how particular features of the local police organization and policy led to different definitions of what constituted 'the problem' of delinquency in the two communities; in their turn, these official definitions were reflected in the very different patterns of official statistics in the two otherwise comparable cities. Cicourel's work shows that the variance in official definitions of delinquency and what police officers consider relevant to their understanding of the problem and their dealings with those they define as delinquents should be treated as a basic problem for the researcher. From the deviance perspective the importance of these official definitions lies also in the ways in which they impinge on the official careers of delinquents, for, as suggested earlier, the nature of the deviant's contact with official agencies is one of the most important contingencies in the development of his deviant career; the outcome of the official definition is also reflected in the nature of the public stigma attached to the official offender. These are likely to vary as official definitions and actions vary. It is worth noting that this comprises only a part of Cicourel's contribution, for he is also concerned with issues of more general sociological interest, especially with those processes of negotiation and meaning construction through which members of a group endeavour to make sense of events in which they are involved by imposing commonly understood explanations on ambiguous features of these events. These explanations are invariably based on common-sense understandings or on what everybody in the society or social group is supposed to know and take-for-granted; it is these very taken-for-granted understandings which should be problematic for the sociologist. The latter must also attempt constantly to call into question his own taken-for-granted assumptions about the phenomenon which he investigates and the implicit rules he typically uses in interpreting these.

It seems that the recent studies investigating delinquency from a stance more or less in harmony with the deviance perspective have both widened and narrowed the focus of investigation. The focus has been widened by incorporating the study of the processes of social control, thereby raising questions which touch upon the fields of political sociology and the sociology of law; at the same time the focus has been narrowed by the attention which it draws towards and the importance which it vests in the structure of everyday common-sense meanings of those involved in the production of delinquency, including both those who commit certain acts and those who define this group as delinquent.

So far the discussion has been concerned exclusively with the developments in American sociological writing on delinquency, and these reflect both the practical and analytical concerns of American sociologists. Questions can be raised immediately concerning the relevance of these studies to the understanding of delinquency elsewhere. In terms of the content of American theories and studies, a distinction can be drawn between those aspects of the theories which refer to apparently universal social processes and those which refer to particular features of American society; those referring to general social processes, such as Cicourel's concern with the processes of statistic production, categorization and social typing, would by definition seem to be more likely to provide useful data for cross-cultural comparisons than those referring to the substantive features of one society, such as Miller's discussion of the black family structure or Cloward and Ohlin's discussion of the retreatist sub-culture. Moreover, it is essential to remember that there are gross differences between American and, for example, English society which are closely related to some of the substantive features of American society held to be important in the various theories of delinquency.

Some of the more obvious differences are listed briefly; their relevance to features of the deviance perspective will be clear. Comparing the social structures of American and English societies, there are major differences in the criminal laws of the two societies, for example, in relation to narcotics; there are major differences in the court and penal systems; police and judicial appointments are closely tied to local politics in the United States and are largely free of such ties in England; the educational system is differently organized at every level in terms of structure, content and control; the ethnic structure of the two societies is completely different; the economic bases of the countries differ radically, as does the role of the central government in both the economic and welfare spheres; the actual pattern of physical violence, reflected in the different homicide rates, the private ownership of firearms and the use of firearms by the police is very different; and the role of organized labour in politics is very different in the two countries. All these things suggest that the meanings attached to the basic features of the individuals' social situations, especially to their class and status positions and to their aspirations and life-styles, are also very different. With such gross and overt differences between the two societies in just those areas of fundamental importance to the various delinquency theories, it would be naïve to expect that the simple transfer of an American theory to the English or other situations could make much of a contribution to our under-standing of patterns of English delinquency. Such a transfer is more likely to mystify than to clarify.

In the only study which has attempted to investigate the relevance of American sub-cultural theory to the English situation, Downes (1966), in his research in East London, concluded that there was little evidence to support Cohen's reaction formation thesis, although there was some evidence for an 'umbrella' or 'parent' sub-culture with a variety of heterogeneous offsprings which was generally supportive of delinquency. There was even less evidence of Cloward and Ohlin's three types, although the subsequent rise in drug dependency among lower-working-class boys both in the area where he did his research and in other neighbourhoods might require a modification of his conclusions on the re-treatist response. Downes argued that a large group of inner urban working-class boys start off in a delinquency-prone life situation; dissociated from the values of school and later alienated from work, the boys indulge in occasional delinquencies as a peripheral leisure activity to manufacture excitement no longer provided by traditional working-class leisure culture. Downes thus saw delinquency as essentially hedonistic. However, his criticism of the American theories was presented in traditional terms, and he was not con-cerned directly with the issues and problems raised by the

148

deviance perspective; his methodology and restriction to one year's Metropolitan Police statistics, complemented by some informal discussion with older boys living in the area, clearly leaves much to be desired even by conventional standards.

Recent work by Hargreaves and by Phillipson, focusing on the educational system, lends support to and provides useful background data on Cicourel and Kitsuse's analysis of the school as a rate and career producing institution. A study of twenty secondary schools in a London borough showed that they had very large and consistent differences in their official delinquency rates over a seven-year period; these differences could not be explained either in terms of the gross characteristics of the schools nor by differential police organization. Most importantly, it was found that the school rates were partially independent of the delinquency rates of their catchment areas; the high delinquency rate schools did not draw their delinquent pupils disproportionately from high rate neighbourhoods and the low rate schools from low rate neighbourhoods. Some schools seemed to be facilitating the drift into delinquency and others protecting their pupils from it (Phillipson, 1971). This finding is lent support by Hargreaves' study of one secondary school in which he describes the emergence of two kinds of sub-cultures in the school during the third and fourth years, one of which he describes as 'delinquescent'; he shows how these two polar sub-cultures, one conforming to the values of the school and the other negating them, emerged as responses to features of the streaming system, the nature of the curriculum and the types of interaction between teachers and pupils in the different streams (Hargreaves, 1967). These two very different studies, together with Downes' discussion of working class boys' dissociation from the school, point to the importance of subjecting

149

the school to closer investigation in relation to its contribution to the production of delinquent careers.

Apart from Mayhew's vivid descriptions, very little sociological research into delinquency was undertaken in England until after the Second World War, and since that time there has been little on the same scale or of the same theoretical and methodological sophistication (admittedly sometimes misplaced) as the American work. There seem to be two complementary themes in the small number of studies carried out in this country. Firstly, there are those which have followed what may be loosely called a 'neighbourhood' perspective; these have focused on particular cities, towns or areas within them and have analysed their broad socio-economic characteristics and the relationship of these to official patterns of delinquency and crime. Sometimes, as in the case of Mays's work (Mays, 1954) in Liverpool, the focus has been more specifically on the character of delinquent activities of the boys within such areas. In addition to Mays' work, this group includes the studies of Mannheim (1948) in Cambridge, Jones (1958) in Leicester and Morris (1957) in Croydon; Morris' study also contains the best critique of the ecological tradition. Secondly, there are those studies which concentrated more on styles of family life in high delinquency neighbourhoods and include the work of Sprott et al. (1954), Wilson (1962), Kerr (1958) and Spinley (1954), although the last two were only peripherally concerned with delinquency, and the work of Wilson is concerned with a very special group of 'multi-problem' families.

These two broad types of studies converge and complement each other in their general conclusions. The stratum at the bottom of the social class hierarchy seems to possess a culture with idiosyncratic characteristics; often described by the term 'slum culture', one of its features is the general tolerance of a wide range of delinquencies, especially those relating to property. For boys living in such neighbourhoods, the studies seem to suggest, that delinquency is defined as a 'normal phenomenon', as something that everybody does. Family values and the character of family relationships in 'slum culture' provide a supportive framework for the emergence of mundane and intermittent delinquent activities. At the most general level of comparison, the findings of these studies seem to be most akin to Miller's analysis in America.

No study has been concerned with social control processes, nor have there been any attempts in English research to investigate such things as the development of delinquent careers or the emergence of delinquent self-concepts; as English research in the past has very much taken its cues from developments in American thinking, it might be expected that increasing attention will be paid to those issues which are raised by the deviance perspective. Because this perspective is concerned mainly with general social processes rather than with the specific features of a given society, it seems likely that, in spite of the fact that its main architects are American, its application to the study of delinquency in England and other societies will be more relevant than that of specific sub-cultural theories.

A final problem to be faced in generating theories which offer explanations of patterns of delinquency is particularly relevant in the English situation; this is the problem raised earlier of the ahistorical character of most theories. If some neighbourhoods and communities have had high official delinquency rates for at least the last hundred years, as the evidence suggests, then how can sociologists come to terms with this in their interpretations? The problem is raised most acutely for those theories which place greatest emphasis on particular features of the total social structure;

examples of the difficulties faced can be illustrated in the theories of Merton and Cohen. Merton (1963) explains the high official rates of delinquency and crime among the lowest social class groups as a common response to the situation of anomie, the disjunction between goals and legitimate means. One then has to ask at what stage in the society's history did this disjunction occur and for what reasons? Unless it has always been present in the same form, a most unlikely hypothesis, one must provide a different sort of explanation for delinquency and crime occurring prior to the emergence of the disjunction. Since there is this consistency in crime rates in some areas, one needs to know if delinquency and crime in the same neighbourhoods change their meanings for the actors over time as a result of major structural changes. If so, what are these changes and how do they influence the meanings attached to delinquency?

The problem is even more pertinent to Cohen's theory, for he explicitly sets out to account for the *emergence* of the delinquent sub-culture, and, as noted, he does this by seeing delinquency as a reaction formation response of working-class boys to their status frustration; this frustration is seen partly as a result of a conflict in values of two social classes (Cohen, 1955). But a question which Cohen does not consider is: when did this emergence of the sub-culture take place? When did the situation of working-class boys become so frustrating that delinquency was 'discovered' as a solution? Again, one must ask if delinquency has changed its meaning for delinquent boys, for, as Bordua (1961) points out, Cohen's boys, driven to delinquency by status frustration, seem a far cry from Thrasher's boys, who found delinquency a positive source of excitement in an often dull and loosely controlled milieu. If delinquency has changed its meaning so drastically, then

SOCIOLOGICAL INTERPRETATIONS

one wants to know why; again Cohen gives us no clues as
to the kind of major social changes which might have produced such changes in the meaning of delinquency. Not
only is it very difficult to decide which social changes, if
any, impinge on delinquent activity; it is even more difficult
to spell out precisely the relationships between the phenomena and the nature of the influence.

Explanations of delinquency and crime in England face
this problem in an acute way because of the very long-
term consistency in the official delinquency rates of many
neighbourhoods. On the one hand, several explanations
might be required, each related to a specific historical
period; in each period delinquency, while running at
approximately the same official rate and having the same
character as the previous period, might mean different
things to both the delinquents and the controllers; in taking
this approach one would clearly have to explain what the
changes in meaning were due to. On the other hand, one
might offer a general theory which attempted to account
for the historical continuity of the patterns and character
of delinquency but which tried to incorporate particular
social changes into its explanation. If the meanings of delinquency for the community, including the regular delinquents, the occasional delinquents, the miniscule group of
non-delinquents and the social controllers (who may be
delinquents too), have changed, then the sociologist's task
is to account for these changes by showing how, why and
when they occurred. Unfortunately the paucity of the kind
of historical data necessary for such explanations makes
this task very difficult and perhaps in part accounts for
sociologists' failure in the past even to consider these issues.

# 6

# Criminology, sociology, crime and social policy

This chapter discusses some of the implications for social policy of the distinctions made in the first two chapters between traditional criminology and the deviance perspective. The underlying theme is the distinction between a social problem and a sociological problem. The study of crime and delinquency provides an excellent example of the confusions that have arisen in the social sciences over the relationship between social scientific theorizing and research activity, and social policy and political action. Here the stance is taken that a clear distinction can be made between social problems and sociological problems and that an understanding of this distinction is essential if the actual implications of sociological analysis for social action are to be brought to light. The following discussion draws heavily on Schuetz's analysis of common-sense and scientific modes of interpretation (Schuetz, 1967).

For the deviance perspective, as for that general sociological perspective comprising the tradition of subjective interpretation, the main methodological problem is to achieve objective and verifiable knowledge of subjective meaning-structures. To understand how sociologists approach this problem a prerequisite is a clear picture of the way in which the sociologist looks at the world and of the distinctive attitude which he adopts towards it. Schuetz distinguishes between what he calls the system of relevances characterizing man in his practical activities which arise within the 'natural attitude' and the system of relevances characterizing man in his role as scientist; in moving from the natural attitude, which characterizes his stance towards the non-scientific activities of his life and is the stance of members of society in their everyday common-sense activities, to the scientific attitude, the social scientist detaches himself from his biographical situation within the social world. In using the term 'system of relevances', Schuetz is referring to those elements of a social situation which the actor, whether scientist or practical man, selects out as relevant to his project or his course of action; the term can thus be defined and illustrated by the kinds of questions asked by the actor in the course of his project which selectively orient him to particular features within a situation. Schuetz's distinction between a scientific project and a practical project of everyday living, includes the idea that the scientific project or problem, such as that of a sociologist, determines what is relevant for the scientist; the orienting questions which comprise the scientist's system of relevances are quite different from the questions of the practical man. As Schuetz says:

> The theoretical scientist – *qua* scientist, not *qua* human being (which he is, too) – is not involved in the observed situation, which is to him not of practical but merely of cognitive interest. The system of relevances governing commonsense interpretation in everyday life originates in the biographical situation of the observer. By making up his mind to become a scientist the social scientist has replaced his personal biographical situation by what I

shall call ... a scientific situation. The problems with which he has to deal may be quite unproblematic for the human being within the world and vice versa. Any scientific problem is determined by the actual state of the respective science and its solution has to be achieved in accordance with the procedural rules governing this science, which among other things warrant the control and verification of the solution offered. The scientific problem once established alone determines what is relevant for the scientist as well as the conceptual frame of references to be used by him. (Schuetz, 1967, p. 63)

This detachment of the scientist requires a move from involvement in practical activities to distinterested observation of them by the social scientist; the move from the natural attitude also requires him to suspend his belief in many of those things which he had taken-for-granted within it. What was relevant for him in his biographical situation within the natural attitude is irrelevant to his problems as a scientist in the scientific attitude of suspended belief in the world previously taken-for-granted.

Of course, this suspension of belief in the world in the move from the natural attitude is an ideal for the sociologist to aim at rather than a description of what actually happens and is arguably the most difficult feature of the sociological project. As some aspects of his natural attitude inevitably enter into his scientific questions and decisions, the problem for the sociologist is to make explicit his system of relevances and to clarify his assumptions and decisions at every stage of his project. Unless this is done, it may be very difficult to evaluate his work, for many of the values out of which his conceptual and methodological decisions emerged will have remained implicit. The point that Schuetz is making is that the programme for scientific research, that is, what the scientist investigates and how he investigates it, is determined by the scientific quest for certain kinds of truth, the validity and reliability of which are judged in terms of the criteria of scientific method; it is the system of relevances which characterizes the particular discipline of sociology, its concepts, assumptions, theories and methods, that determines what is a problem for the sociologist and not the system of relevances of men in their natural attitudes facing practical problems of living. Schuetz then goes on to develop a programme for sociological analysis within the scientific attitude and suggests what the main components of the social scientist's system of relevance might be. However, in this context it is sufficient to note that, once the scientific problem has been established it is this alone which determines what is relevant and what is not; in the scientific attitude the social scientist will tend to take-for-granted only those things accepted and established by his fellow scientists and those things deemed scientifically irrelevant to his scientific project in hand. If the scientific project shifts in character during the course of investigation, so accordingly does the system of scientific relevances; the different levels of scientific analysis each possess their own systems of relevances, each of which is quite distinct from systems of relevances characterizing the natural attitude.

The distinction between the formation and use of, on the one hand, common-sense constructs and concepts, by means of which we describe and interpret our practical experiences in the natural attitude and, on the other hand, the constructs and concepts of science, further illustrates the difference between the scientific and the natural attitude. Our common-sense constructs arise out of our biographical situations and rest on and take-for-granted a stock of socially approved knowledge; these common-sense constructs have their place within the chains of motives characterizing the everyday activities of men. On the other hand, social scientific constructs and concepts are what Schuetz calls 'second-order constructs' and, as they arise out of scientific problems, are very different from those emerging in the natural attitude to deal with practical problems. The stock of knowledge taken-for-granted by the scientist is that knowledge which comprises his discipline and which includes a generally agreed body of concepts and methods for forming scientifically useful concepts; what he takes-for-granted as a scientist and what he calls into question are quite independent of the accepted values, beliefs and interests of men in their practical activities. If the main aim of sociology is to achieve objective knowledge of subjective meaning structures, then this task carries with it structures of relevances and a stock of taken-for-granted scientific knowledge which are inevitably completely different from those which men bring to bear on their practical activities in the world, for the latter's aims arise out of their biographical situations. The world would rapidly grind to a halt if men started in large numbers to adopt the social scientific attitude of suspension of certain kinds of belief in their social worlds.

An illustration of the importance of this distinction can be given by elaborating the comparison between traditional criminology and the deviance perspective. Some of the main characteristics of the structures of relevances and the stocks of taken-for-granted knowledge of the two perspectives can be contrasted with special reference to their implications for practical action in relation to crime and delinquency.

In the critique of traditional criminology presented in chapter 1, particular stress was laid on its normative character; its subject matter was defined by criteria external to the discipline, that is, by social definitions of what constituted crime and of the ways in which crime was a social problem requiring positive social action against it. Criminology was seen to be defined by and therefore inextricably bound up with society's definitions and problems; in effect criminology was, and still is, the servant, firstly, of the political values which define crime and the criminal as immediately problematic for society and, secondly, of the personal values of the working criminologists, who broadly accept these political values and work within them and whose research work is directed to the practical everyday problems of penal systems.

The system of relevances characterizing criminology is one which is congruent with that of politicians and members of society in their natural attitudes: criminology shares with the public the common-sense definitions of crime and the criminal as major social problems. It does not suspend its belief in the socially shared assumptions about the pathological features of crime but accepts these assumptions and works within them; in so doing it allows these common-sense assumptions and definitions, which emerge from and lie within the natural attitude, to determine its problems of investigation. The problems addressed by criminology are handed to it by politicians and pressure groups or arise out of the personal values of the criminologists themselves within their natural attitudes and are not determined by a scientific system of relevances.

If this is the general structure of relevances within which criminologists operate, what are the typical components of their stock of taken-for-granted knowledge? Clearly, this knowledge, too, is largely non-scientific, for it lies within the structure of relevances just mentioned. The following seem to be the pervasive, implicit and taken-for-granted assumptions in much criminological research and writing. Some of these assumptions are inter-related and are rarely found on their own but imply each other. Firstly, there is the assumption that there are universal causes of crime which can be located through criminological research methods which in their turn rely heavily on the use and logic of the statistical method. This is closely related to another prime feature of criminology, namely, its division of the population into two groups, criminals and non-criminals, the assumption being that the causes of crime can be located by finding factors which significantly differentiate the two groups. Thirdly, and growing out of the first two assumptions, is the implicit notion in prescriptive criminological writing that if the causes of crime can be located by the study of individual criminals, then the prevention of crime can best be achieved by doing something to these same individuals. Fourthly, in analysing patterns of crime in society, although lip service is generally paid to the limitations of official statistics as measures of the 'problem', nevertheless they are still typically used as indices of trends in crime.

An illustration of the difficulties of analysis which these assumptions bring and which are typically not recognized by criminologists themselves can be found by a more detailed analysis of the third assumption concerning criminological views on crime prevention and the change of criminals. A common theme underlying the work of criminologists who investigate politically defined problems of the penal system is that of increasing its rationality by evaluating its activities; this rationality is defined in terms which attempt to relate limited penal ends to more effective means. For example, the main ends of the courts' sentencing activities are taken by criminologists, often quite explicitly, to be the reduction of recidivism, that is, preventing officially defined offenders from committing further crimes and deterring potential offenders; both Wootton

(1963) and Wilkins (1965) propose this as the main aim of the sentencing process. Having accepted this as the main aim, criminologists typically proceed in their evaluative research as if it was the only aim of the penal system and develop techniques for measuring how effective court sentences and subsequent penal practices are in achieving this end with the processed offenders. The belief which presumably underlies this kind of research is that the evaluation techniques used will provide the society with better, more rational data on how its penal system is working and will enable it to make informed modifications of the system; findings from such investigations might lead eventually to political decisions affecting sentencing practice or changing the nature of penal regimes.

The assumption of a single main aim in the penal system on which such writings rest is such a simplification of the complexities of the ambiguous and conflicting ethical principles, justifications and meanings underlying contemporary penal activities, that it grossly distorts the realities faced by courts and penal institutions. The distortion is more likely to confuse than to clarify practical actions within the penal system; insofar as the decisions and activities of penal institutions reflect other aims and meanings apart from the reduction of recidivism, such as retribution, protection of society or individual atonement, or insofar as they take on the symbolic meanings of punishment suggested in chapter 3, the explicit limitation to a single aim in evaluative studies fails to come to terms with the actual meanings of penal activities.

The main implications for social policy of criminology's relevance structure and stock of taken-for-granted knowledge are politically comfortable and convenient. They suggest that the pursuit of criminological research and the implementation of changes in the penal system based upon its findings will bring an increased rationality into penal practices; the underlying assumption appears to be that this rationality will bring increasingly effective crime prevention and criminal treatment procedures. This optimistic view of the values of criminological research is likely to find general support among politicians and the public not only because it shares their definition of crime as a social problem but also because it poses no threat to existing social institutions and interest groups. The narrow views of causation and treatment imply that the problem can be effectively dealt with by minor modifications here and there to parts of the system, in particular by modifications of parts of the penal system. Thus, by taking-for-granted and working within societal definitions of the problem, criminology becomes a highly conservative and therefore politically convenient discipline, while criminologists themselves are servants of social policy who occasionally contribute to minor innovations in policy.

A word of caution is in order here. Whilst this may seem to be an indictment of criminology from a sociological standpoint, it is not intended to suggest that the presence of criminologists in the social policy-creating institutions cannot be reasonably justified in terms of conventional political values or that there are no aspects of criminological research that are of value to a society, such as providing it with more information about its practical penal problems. The important thing is rather to recognize the value bases of criminology and the implications of these for its wider claims both to scientific status and to providing the effective answers to a society's crime problem. Contemporary societies do justify the employment of criminologists, and their data is used in political decision-making; however, from a sociological perspective, their contributions must be judged according to criteria other than those used to justify criminology's narrow views of causation and treatment. For example, an important measure of their contribution would be how far their partial and limited view of rationality is accepted and acted upon in a given penal system and in what ways political decisions about the penal system are affected by the data which criminologists produce. Insofar as criminologists subscribe to a view of rationality in penal decision-making, however partial it is, and insofar as rationality is a tenet of humanism, as a group in the service of social policy criminologists can be viewed as a small humanizing force. Their role seems to be to recommend penal changes on the basis of a limited ethic of evaluation, and in doing this they contribute to the growth of certain kinds of rationality in social policy.

The deviance perspective contrasts markedly with traditional criminology both in its system of relevances and its stock of taken-for-granted knowledge; consequently it also carries with it different implications for social and penal policy. Its system of relevances, that is, its basic orienting questions about the phenomenon of crime, derives from its place in the sociological tradition of subjective interpretation. This broad tradition rests on assumptions about man and social life which have very particular conceptual and methodological implications, as was pointed out in chapter 2. The deviance perspective's problems are therefore defined not by societal definitions of what the problem is and what should be investigated but by a particular conceptual tradition in sociology. We have already seen that this tradition places the study of crime in the context of deviance from shared rules, emphasizes the interactional and dynamic character of social relations with its related focus on the interaction between rule breakers and social controllers, and is methodologically founded on the study of structures of subjective meaning. These comprise some of the main features of the deviance perspective's system of relevances and indicate the kind of problems addressed by it. The orientation lays claim to certain kinds of objectivity and validity which are very different in character from those claimed by criminology; the criteria of validity are derived from its techniques of concept formation, theory construction and methods of investigation, all of which differ considerably from those of traditional criminology. In their discussions of sociological interpretations both Schuetz and Gibson Winter – whose concern is the relationship between social science, ethics and social policy (Winter, 1966) – conclude that ultimately the validity of sociological interpretations must rest on there being direct continuity between the sociologist's models or interpretations (his 'second-order constructs') and the lived experiences of the actors whose actions he is interpreting. Sociological interpretations must both make sense to and illumine the understanding of the actors studied by sociologists. The criteria of objectivity and validity in criminology rest largely on its adherence to narrow interpretations of statistical method, while the meaning of its explanations to those studied is never mentioned or recognized as a problem.

Methodologically the two approaches could hardly be further apart. In particular, the different ways they view the deviant or official offender are indicative of their polar systems of relevances. In criminology, a deviant act is typically seen as a product or symptom of underlying causes, which in contemporary criminology are multifactorial in character; the deviant act is rarely viewed as important in itself in terms of its subjective meaning to its author, rather it is taken to be symptomatic of some underlying pathology. In the deviance perspective exactly the opposite approach is followed, and the subjective meanings of men's actions are in themselves the central concern of the sociologist. As Matza (1969) has pointed out in *Becoming Deviant*, the adoption of a correctional stance towards the deviant, which characterizes criminology and much earlier sociology, precludes the possibility of using one of the very methodological devices which is central to the deviance perspective in its quest for subjective understanding. This, very simply, is empathy, or the ability effectively to take the role of the deviant or criminal and see the world through his eyes. If a correctional stance is adopted, it becomes very difficult for the investigator to empathize with the deviant and to appreciate his subjective meaning. The correctional stance thus reinforces the view that deviant acts are basically pathological because it maintains a distance between the criminologist and his subject which precludes empathy. Following Berger's suggestion that sociologists attempt to achieve 'ecstasy' in their interpretations by dropping or standing outside their common-sense assumptions, so in attempting to understand the subjective meaning of deviant acts must the sociologist suspend his conventional abhorrence or other emotion and attempt to take the deviant's perspective of the world (Berger, 1968). As Berger (1968, p. 171) says: 'Only by stepping outside the taken-for-granted routines of society is it possible for us to confront the human condition without comforting mystifications.' Apart from the guides laid down by the scientific rules of procedure and the existing conceptual apparatus of the ongoing tradition, the other main feature of the sociological relevance system is the suspension of belief in common-sense values concerning the penal system. This involves a move from the natural attitude towards punishment and treatment to an attitude of radical doubt achieved through 'ecstasy'.

The components of the stock of taken-for-granted sociological knowledge which lie within its structure of relevances contrast markedly with those of criminology and, like the latter's, are also inter-related. Firstly, it is taken-for-granted that the content and pattern of crime and the responses to it are relative to time and place, so that the search for universal causes is inappropriate: there may be common processes in very different societies, such as deviance from enforceable rules, attempts to control it or public rituals for stigmatizing the deviant person, but the actual content of these processes will inevitably differ very considerably. Thus, while the sociologist will need to analyse the actual content of rules, their enforcement and deviance from them within a society, if he is to provide a sociologically adequate interpretation of them, his main concern is to clarify sociological understanding of the social processes which are common to different societies. Secondly, the assumption, discussed in detail in chapter 3, that crime and deviance and their punishment are normal phenomena in society and are fundamental features of social life, is central to sociological analysis of these phenomena. A recognition of normality again contrasts strongly with the natural attitude stance of criminology, which views crime as inherently pathological and problematic. It also leads directly to a third taken-for-granted tenet – that crime cannot be eliminated from society. Indeed the direct implication of this for social policy is that all the preventive and treatment programmes deriving from criminological research are doomed to failure; their failure rests, firstly, in their basic assumptions concerning the possibility of prevention and the viability of treatment and, subsequently, in the targets they choose for their preventive and treatment actions, that is, the limitation of their actions to officially designated offenders. A further assumption of the sociological perspective is that the common-sense measures of a society's patterns of crime and deviance, its official statistics, cannot be used for this purpose except in very isolated cases; official data are viewed as the product of a series of interactions between located offenders and social control agencies and as such they are to be seen as indices of organizational behaviour rather than measures of deviance. These are some of the main components of the stock of taken-for-granted sociological knowledge about crime and deviance: placed in their context of the sociological structure of relevances, they direct sociologists' attention to very different analytical problems from those tackled by criminology.

The implications of this sociological stance towards its subject matter are very different from those of criminology. From the viewpoint of criminology and the natural attitude they are pessimistic and politically uncomfortable in their implication that to radically alter the pattern of crime in society would require fundamental and large-scale changes in the social structure; simply tampering with isolated parts of the whole, as in the practices resulting from criminology, has no effect on patterns of crime and criminality, for these are bound up with the essential social processes and conditions of life characterizing a society. Indeed, even if large-scale structural changes were to occur and social relationships were radically reorganized, for whatever reasons, crime and deviance, being intrinsic to social organization, would not disappear but would simply change their form; there would still be acts defined as deviant and would still be attempts to control them.

It must be made clear that these sociological assumptions cannot in themselves be taken as support either for undertaking the kinds of changes required to alter the character of crime or for maintaining the political status quo. They simply represent a particular perspective towards the phenomenon of crime, and the value conclusions drawn from them by members of society in their natural attitudes and by sociologists, too, when they return from the scientific to the natural attitude, will depend on their background relevances and stocks of taken-for-granted social knowledge in their natural attitudes.

If sociological problems are distinguishable from social problems by virtue of their origins in different relevance systems, can the relationship between sociological writing and research and problems of social policy be clarified? In terms of social policy the particular problem of crime is largely a problem of dealing with individual criminals and delinquents; whilst they may be discussed in more general terms in political debate, the everyday problems of the penal and welfare systems centre on how to deal with particular individuals. The solutions to these practical problems emerge from the relevance systems of the natural attitude and include considerations of economic and political expedience, strongly felt moral beliefs and unarticulated taken-for-granted assumptions about the efficacy of punishment in changing and deterring offenders. A feature of sociology's relevance system, the fact that its theories, models and constructs are concerned with the *typical* features of action and meaning, immediately points up the problem of relating sociological conceptualization to the world of practical action. Sociological typifications of action and meaning, Schuetz's 'second-order constructs', by definition are removed from the common-sense, practical activities of members of society; these typifications are a product of certain kinds of reflection by sociologists on the common-sense world. This would suggest that the main relationship between sociological reflection about the world and practical activities in the world lies, as Gibson Winter proposes, in sociology's ability to clarify these practical activities (Winter, 1966).

Insofar as sociological data and interpretations are valid, that is, insofar as they are accurate depictions from the standpoint of sociological abstraction of the way things are in the world, they do not, in themselves, support any common-sense interest or value position. Sociological evidence can be used to support the cases of those desiring social changes and those desiring to preserve the status quo because each group selects out from sociological data that which supports its own case. An example of this can be found in the debate about the efficacy of capital punishment. Whilst sociologists have demonstrated that the murder rate of a society seems to be independent of its use of capital punishment, no study can deny or confirm that in a few cases it may have acted as a deterrent; nor can standard sociological measurement techniques for comparing and evaluating the deterrent effect of capital punishment deal with the conflicting desire for retribution held by many members of a society. The debate therefore becomes, in the last analysis, one of clashing moral viewpoints in which sociological evidence can be used by both sides in the debate; obviously such evidence is most likely to appeal to those who in their natural attitudes share some of the assumptions of sociology. Perhaps it is only in those cases where a society claims to be doing one thing and actually acts in a way directly opposed to these claims that the sociologist can act in some sense as the society's moral conscience. An illustration of this is Myrdal's *The American Dilemma*, where he analyses the contradictions between the fundamental American beliefs in freedom and equality and the social position of the black man in American society (Myrdal, 1944). The contribution of sociology, then, through its clarification of man's practical activities, is that it can help the members of a society to pose their own dilemmas more clearly and acutely.

With issues where there is overlap between sociologists' analytical interests and the common-sense societal definitions of a social problem, such as crime, mental health or poverty, particular difficulties emerge for sociologists. Because these are important social problems, the sociologist whose work touches on such areas is subject to political pressures from interested groups which may try to influence both the content and the methods of his study. The sociologist's dilemma may be exacerbated by the fact that he often receives financial and other supports for his projects from groups which have a direct practical interest in the issues which he investigates and the products of his research. In such situations the onus is placed on the sociologist to be as explicit as possible in his descriptions and explanations of his assumptions, his methodology, his concepts and his findings simply because groups are likely to use his findings to support their own value interests. The sociologists's responsibility here is not only towards those who have helped to finance him but also, and more importantly, towards the people who have been the subjects of his investigation, for their lives may be changed as a result of the social uses of his research. In the case of those defined as deviant by the society, many changes in official policy may drastically affect their lives, so that sometimes the sociologist may feel it necessary to conceal certain sorts of information given to him in good faith by deviant characters. These dual and sometimes conflicting responsibilities can create considerable dilemmas for sociologists in the field of deviance and social problems.

A concluding point in relation to those dilemmas can be made in considering the relationship between the sociologist, his research findings and his mundane membership of a society and his consequent engagement in its common-sense, practical activities. Whether or not the sociologist

conducting a piece of research in an area also defined as a
social problem decides to follow up through personal political action what he defines as the implications of his findings
will depend on his personal values. The particular implications which he selects out for follow-up in personal action
will rest not on his sociological knowledge but on his own
view of the world in the natural attitude; in his common-
sense perspective on the world, his sociological perspective
is simply one among many interests and values, so that his
move from the scientific attitude back to the natural attitude brings back into play his common-sense understanding
of the world and re-creates the background relevances necessary for his political action or inaction.

# Suggestions for further reading

The importance of placing the study of crime and delinquency in a general sociological context has been stressed
throughout this book. It requires the investigator and the
student to relate the substantive questions asked about
crime to the general conceptual and methodological problems of sociology. Questions must be framed in terms of and
placed within the context of sociological rather than social
problems. Few sociologists working in the area of crime
and delinquency have consistently made this distinction in
their work, with the result that the bulk of written
material on crime is 'social problem' oriented. The reading
recommendations made here are limited, with the exception of those relating to traditional criminology, to
writers who tried to adopt a consistently sociological
approach to the problems which interested them and whose
work forms direct links with the mainstream of sociology.

The development of traditional criminology has been well
documented from within by criminologists, the most comprehensive work being that of Mannheim (1965); in addition, Vold (1958) provides a succinct critique of the various
'schools' of criminological explanation. The work of S. and
E. Glueck (1950, 1964) epitomizes the methods and assumptions of traditional criminology, and one of their studies

and a collection of their papers should give the flavour of their approach. Two articles by Tappan (1947) and Sellin (1938), reprinted in a book of readings (Wolfgang, Savitz and Johnston, 1962), provide an early example of the debate between the traditional legalistic approach and the sociological orientation. A paper by C. Wright Mills (1963a) in which he criticizes the value assumptions of 'social pathologists' was an early attempt to draw an analytical distinction between sociological and social problems.

Within the deviance perspective there are very few writers who have contributed integrated and detailed approaches. Of these the most convincing and comprehensive is Lofland (1969), who presents a carefully documented conceptual approach to the analysis of deviance. Among the other contributions, Matza (1969), provides an excellent discussion of the emergence of the deviance perspective within sociology, while Becker in his own book and in his introduction to a book of readings raises many of the issues and introduces some of the concepts which have been touched upon in this book (Becker, 1963, 1964). In his early work, Lemert (1951) first raised some of the ideas which are now taken-for-granted within the deviance perspective and which he himself elaborated subsequently (Lemert, 1967). More specifically, in relation to crime rather than deviance in general, Gibbons (1968) has presented an integrated approach to the study of criminality which centres on the concepts of role and career; many empirical studies which lend support to this approach can be found in Clinard and Quinney's book of readings (Clinard and Quinney, 1967). Examples of sociological approaches to other forms of social deviance can be found in Scheff's analysis of mental illness (Scheff, 1966) and Lindesmith's work on drug addiction (Lindesmith, 1965).

Of the vast amount written on juvenile delinquency,

173

mainly American, the following is a selection of the best of the theoretical and empirical work: the early 'classics' of Thrasher (1963) and Shaw (1930, 1931) illustrate what can be gained from two contrasting methods, observation and studies of the delinquent career. Downes (1966) draws together the strands leading up to the sub-cultural approach and provides a detailed appraisal of American and English research. Matza's excellent critique of previous approaches to explaining delinquency and his own theory (Matza, 1964), together with Cicourel's study (Cicourel, 1968) illustrate the movement to integrate the study of delinquency into general sociology. The researches of Short and Strodtbeck (1965) and Chein *et al.* (1964), in two contrasting fields of peer group life, gang delinquency and drug use, illustrate the benefits of careful fieldwork.

More generally, the theoretical and methodological assumptions of this approach are most succinctly and lucidly presented by Schuetz in the essays contained in the first volume of his *Collected Papers* (Schuetz, 1967); the papers in Part 1 of this volume present an excellent intro-duction to the perspective adopted in the present book. The implications of Schuetz's approach for general metho-dology in sociology are spelled out by Cicourel (1964), and in a more complex theoretical discussion, Gibson Winter (1966) surveys the relationship between different sociolo-gical perspectives and practical social action.

The methodological style of observation, participant or otherwise, which is most appropriate to the deviance pers-pective, is well illustrated by the studies of Whyte (1966), Liebow (1967) and Polsky (1967). Severyn Bruyn (1966) makes out the most convincing and persuasive case for this research style. The book of readings compiled by McCall and Simmons (1969) complements Bruyn's work, although many of the criticisms made by writers in this book are done from the standpoint of traditional methodology.

*Readings*
There is now an abundance of American readings in the fields of deviance and crime which brings together a wide range of papers and extracts from books. Some of these books of readings are of particular value to English readers because they contain papers which may otherwise be difficult to obtain. These readings inevitably reflect the personal tastes and interests of their compilers, so that any recommendation is somewhat arbitrary; moreover, because of the paucity of really good papers, there is often considerable overlap between the readings. However, apart from these limitations and the inevitable American bias of the books, the following have been carefully compiled and present some of the best papers written in the field of deviance:

CRESSEY, D. R. and WARD, D. A., eds. (1969), *Delinquency, Crime and Social Process*, New York: Harper & Row.
DINITZ, S., DYNES, R. R. and CLARKE, A. C., eds. (1969), *Deviance*, London: Oxford University Press.
LEFTON, M., SKIPPER, J. K. and MCCAGHY, C. H., eds. (1968), *Approaches to Deviance*, New York: Appleton-Century-Crofts.
RUBINGTON, E. and WEINBERG, M. S., eds. (1968), *Deviance: the interactionist perspective*, New York: Macmillan.

Specifically in the field of delinquency Giallombardo's book contains a wide range of material:

GIALLOMBARDO, R., ed. (1966), *Juvenile Delinquency*, New York: John Wiley.

The Harper Row 'Social Problems' series contains a collection of shorter books of readings on particular types of social deviance such as mental illness, alcoholism, narcotic addiction and middle-class juvenile delinquency.

The only book of readings dealing specifically with the English situation from an explicitly sociological perspective is:

> WILES, P. and CARSON, W. G., eds. (1971), *Crime and Delinquency in Britain: Sociological Readings*, London: Martin Robertson.

*Journals*
The interests of traditional criminology are represented by:

> *British Journal of Criminology*
> *Journal of the Howard League*
> *Journal of Offender Therapy*

Sociological papers on crime and delinquency are much more widely scattered across the range of American and English sociology journals. However, two journals are of special importance in this area; the main focus of the American journal *Social Problems* is the field of social deviance, and it contains a wide range of articles and research reports relating to this area; another American journal, *Social Forces*, although more wide-ranging in its sociological subject matter, frequently contains articles in the field of social deviance.

# Bibliography

BECKER, H. S. (1963), *Outsiders: studies in the sociology of deviance*, New York: Free Press.

BECKER, H. S., ed. (1964), *The Other Side*, New York: Free Press.

BERGER, P. (1968), *Invitation to Sociology*, London: Penguin Books.

BERNSTEIN, B. (1960), 'Language and Social Class', *British Journal of Sociology*, Vol. XI, pp. 271-6.

BORDUA, D. (1961), 'Delinquent Sub-cultures: sociological interpretations of gang delinquency', *Annals of the American Academy of Political and Social Science*, Vol. 338 (November), pp. 119-36. Reprinted in Wolfgang, Savitz and Johnston, eds. (1962).

BORDUA, D., ed. (1967), *The Police: six essays*, New York: John Wiley.

BRUYN, S. T. (1966), *The Human Perspective in Sociology*, Englewood Cliffs, N. J.: Prentice-Hall.

BURGESS, E. (1942), Introduction to C. R. Shaw and H. D. McKay, *Juvenile Delinquency and Urban Areas*, University of Chicago Press.

CHAPMAN, D. (1968), *Sociology and the Stereotype of the Criminal*, London: Tavistock Publications.

CHEIN, I., GERARD, D. L., LEE, R. S. and ROSENFELD, E. (1964), *The Road to H*, London: Tavistock Publications.

CICOUREL, A. V. (1964), *Method and Measurement in Sociology*, New York: Free Press.

177

BIBLIOGRAPHY

CICOUREL, A. V. (1968), *The Social Organization of Juvenile Justice*, New York: John Wiley.

CICOUREL, A. V. and KISUSE, J. I. (1963a), 'A Note on the Use of Official Statistics', *Social Problems*, No. 11 (Fall), pp. 131-9.

CICOUREL, A. V. and KITSUSE, J. I. (1963b), *The Educational Decision Makers*, Indianapolis: Bobbs-Merrill.

COHEN, A. (1955), *Delinquent Boys*, Chicago: Free Press.

COHEN, A. (1966), *Deviance and Control*, Englewood Cliffs, N.J.: Prentice-Hall.

CLINARD, M., ed. (1964), *Anomie and Deviant Behaviour*, New York: Free Press.

CLINARD, M. and QUINNEY, R., eds. (1967), *Criminal Behaviour Systems*, New York: Holt, Rinehart and Winston.

CLOWARD, R. and OHLIN, L. (1960), *Delinquency and Opportunity*, Chicago: Free Press.

CRESSEY, D. (1953), *Other People's Money*, Chicago: Free Press.

DINITZ, S., DYNES, R. R. and CLARKE, A. C., eds. (1969), *Deviance*, London: Oxford University Press.

DOWNES, D. M. (1966), *The Delinquent Solution*, London: Routledge & Kegan Paul.

DURKHEIM, E. (1950), *The Rules of Sociological Method*, Chicago: Free Press.

DURKHEIM, E. (1951), *Suicide*, Chicago: Free Press.

DURKHEIM, E. (1961), *Moral Education*, New York: Free Press.

DURKHEIM, E. (1965), *Division of Labour*, New York: Free Press.

ERICKSON, K. T. (1962), 'Notes on the Sociology of Deviance', *Social Problems* (Spring), in Becker, ed., pp. 307-14. Reprinted (1964).

FRIEDLANDER, K. (1947), *The Psychoanalytic Approach to Juvenile Delinquency*, New York: International Universities Press.

GARFINKEL, H. (1956), 'Conditions of Successful Degradation Ceremonies', *American Journal of Sociology*, Vol. LXI (March), pp. 420-4.

GENET, J. (1964), *The Thief's Journal*, New York: Grove Press.

GERTH, H. H. and MILLS, C. W. (1961), *Character and Social Structure*, London: Routledge & Kegan Paul.

GIALLOMBARDO, R., ed. (1966), *Juvenile Delinquency*, New York: John Wiley.

GIBBONS, D. (1968), *Society, Crime and Criminal Careers*, Englewood Cliffs, N.J.: Prentice-Hall.

GLASER, D. (1964), *The Effectiveness of a Prison and Parole System*, Indianapolis: Bobbs-Merrill.

GLOVER, E. (1960), *The Roots of Crime*, London: Imago Publishing.

GLUECK, S. and E. (1950), *Unravelling Juvenile Delinquency*, Cambridge, Mass.: Harvard University Press.

GLUECK, S. and E. (1969), *Ventures in Criminology*, London: Tavistock Publications.

GOFFMAN, E. (1963), *Behaviour in Public Places*, New York: Free Press.

GOLD, M. (1963), *Status Forces in Delinquent Boys*, Ann Arbor: University of Michigan Press.

HALMOS, P., ed. (1965), *Sociological Studies in the British Penal Services*, Keele University Press.

HARGREAVES, D. (1967), *Social Relations in a Secondary School*, London: Routledge & Kegan Paul.

HOME OFFICE (1967), *Criminal Statistics for England and Wales*, London: H.M.S.O.

HOME OFFICE (1969), *Criminal Statistics for England and Wales*, London: H.M.S.O.

JONES, H. (1958), 'Approaches to an Ecological Study', *British Journal of Delinquency*, Vol. VIII, No. 4 (April), pp. 277-93.

KERR, M. (1958), *The People of Ship Street*, London: Routledge & Kegan Paul.

KOBRIN, S. (1959), 'The Chicago Area Project', *Annals of the American Academy of Political and Social Science*, Vol.

322 (March), pp. 20-9. Reprinted in Giallombardo, ed. (1966).

LEFTON, M., SKIPPER, J. K. and MCCAGHY, C. H., eds. (1968), *Approaches to Deviance*, New York: Appleton-Century-Crofts.

LEMERT, E. (1951), *Social Pathology*, New York: McGraw-Hill.

LEMERT, E. (1958), 'The Behaviour of the Systematic Cheque Forger', *Social Problems*, No. 6 (Fall), pp. 141-9. Reprinted in Lemert (1967).

LEMERT, E. (1967), *Human Deviance, Social Problems and Social Control*, Englewood Cliffs, N.J.: Prentice-Hall.

LIEBOW, E. (1967), *Tally's Corner*, Boston: Little, Brown.

LINDESMITH, A. (1965), *The Addict and the Law*, New York: Vintage Books.

LINDESMITH, A. and LEVIN, Y. (1937), 'The Lombrosian Myth in Criminology', *American Journal of Sociology*, Vol. XLII (March), pp. 653-71.

LOFLAND, J. (1969), *Deviance and Identity*, Englewood Cliffs, N.J.: Prentice-Hall.

MCCALL, G. J. and SIMMONS, J. L., eds. (1969), *Issues in Participant Observation*, Reading, Mass.: Addison-Wesley.

MCCORD, W. and J. (1959), *Origins of Crime: a new evaluation of the Cambridge-Somerville Youth Study*, New York: Columbia University Press.

MANNHEIM, H. (1948), *Juvenile Delinquency in an English Middletown*, London: Kegan Paul, Trench, Trubner.

MANNHEIM, H. (1965), *Comparative Criminology*, Vols. I and II, Routledge & Kegan Paul.

MANNHEIM, H. and WILKINS, L. (1955), *Prediction Methods in Relation to Borstal Training*, London: H.M.S.O.

MARTIN, J. P. (1962), *Offenders as Employees*, London: Macmillan.

MATZA, D. (1964), *Delinquency and Drift*, New York: John Wiley.

MATZA, D. (1969), *Becoming Deviant*, Englewood Cliffs, N.J.: Prentice-Hall.

MAYHEW, H. (1862), *London Labour and the London Poor*, Vol. IV. Edited and published as *London's Underworld*, London: Spring Books (1966).

MAYS, J. B. (1954), *Growing Up in the City*, Liverpool University Press.

MEAD, G. H. (1918), 'The Psychology of Punitive Justice', *American Journal of Sociology*, Vol. XXIII, pp. 577-602. Reprinted in A. Reck, ed., *Mead: Selected Writings*, New York: Bobbs-Merrill (1964).

MEAD, G. H. (1934), *Mind, Self and Society*. Reprinted by University of Chicago Press (1967).

MERTON, R. K. (1949), *Social Theory and Social Structure*. Reprinted New York: Free Press (1963).

MILLER, W. B. (1958), 'Lower Class Life as a Generating Milieu of Gang Delinquency', *Journal of Social Issues*, Vol. XIV, No. 3, pp. 5-19. Reprinted in Giallombardo, ed. (1966).

MILLER, W. B. (1962), 'The Impact of a Total-Community Delinquency Control Project', *Social Problems*, Vol. X, No. 2 (Fall), pp. 168-91. Reprinted in Giallombardo, ed. (1966).

MILLS, C. W. (1963a), 'The Professional Ideology of Social Pathologists' in *Power, Politics and People*, New York: Oxford University Press.

MILLS, C. W. (1963b), 'Situated Actions and Vocabularies of Motive' in *Power, Politics and People*, New York: Oxford University Press.

MORRIS, T. (1957), *The Criminal Area*, London: Routledge & Kegan Paul.

MORRISON, A. (1896), *A Child of the Jago*. Reprinted London: Penguin Books (1946).

MYRDAL, G. (1944), *An American Dilemma*, New York: Harper.

PARK, R. E. with BURGESS, E. W., MACKENZIE, R. D. and WIRTH, L. (1925), *The City*, University of Chicago Press.

PERKS COMMITTEE (1967), *Report*, London: H.M.S.O.

BIBLIOGRAPHY

PHILLIPSON, C. M. (1971), 'Juvenile Delinquency and the School' in P. Wiles and W. G. Carson, eds. (1971).

PILIAVIN, I. and BRIAR, S. (1964), 'Police Encounters with Juveniles', *American Journal of Sociology*, Vol. LXX (September), pp. 206-14. Reprinted in Giallombardo, ed. (1966).

POLSKY, N. (1967), *Hustlers, Beats and Others*, Chicago: Aldine.

POWER, M. J. (1962), 'Trends in Juvenile Delinquency', *The Times*, (9 August).

POWER, M. J. (1965), 'An Attempt to Identify at First Appearance before the Courts those at Risk of Becoming Persistent Juvenile Offenders', *Proceedings of Royal Society of Medicine*, Vol. LVII, No. 9 (September), pp. 704-5.

RUBINGTON, E. and WEINBERG, M. S., eds. (1968), *Deviance: the interactionist perspective*, New York: Macmillan.

SAVITZ, L. (1967), *Dilemmas in Criminology*, New York: McGraw-Hill.

SCHEFF, T. J. (1966), *Being Mentally Ill*, Chicago: Aldine Publishing.

SCHUETZ, A. (1967), *Collected Papers*, Vol. I., The Hague: Martinus Nijhoff.

SCHUR, E. M. (1965), *Crimes without Victims*, Englewood Cliffs, N.J.: Prentice-Hall.

SELLIN, T. (1938), *Culture, Conflict and Crime*, New York: Social Science Research Council, Bulletin 71, pp. 17-32. Reprinted as 'A Sociological Approach to the Study of Crime Causation' in Wolfgang, Savitz and Johnston, eds. (1962).

SHAW, C. R. (1930), *The Jack Roller*. Reprinted by University of Chicago Press (1966).

SHAW, C. R. (1931), *The Natural History of a Delinquent Career*, Philadelphia: Albert Saifer.

SHAW, C. R. and MCKAY, H. D. (1942), *Juvenile Delinquency in Urban Areas*, University of Chicago Press.

SHORT, J. F. and STRODTBECK, F. L. (1965), *Group Process*

*and Gang Delinquency*, University of Chicago Press.

SKOLNICK, J. H. (1966), *Justice without Trial*, New York: John Wiley.

SPERGEL, I. (1964), *Racketville, Slumtown and Haulberg*, University of Chicago Press.

SPINLEY, B. (1954), *The Deprived and the Privileged*, London: Routledge & Kegan Paul.

SPROTT, W. J. H., JEPHCOTT, P. and CARTER, M. (1954), 'The Social Background of Delinquency', University of Nottingham (unpublished).

STINCHCOMBE, A. (1963), 'Institutions of Privacy in the Determination of Police Administrative Practice', *American Journal of Sociology*, Vol. LXIX (September), pp. 150-60.

SUTHERLAND, E. H. (1949), *White Collar Crime*, New York: Holt, Rinehart and Winston.

SUTHERLAND, E. H. and CRESSEY, D. (1960), *Principles of Criminology*, New York: Lippincott.

TANNENBAUM, F. (1938), *Crime and the Community*, Boston: Ginn.

TAPPAN, P. (1947), 'Who is the Criminal', *American Sociological Review* (Feb.), p. 12. Reprinted in Wolfgang, Savitz and Johnston, eds. (1962).

THOMAS, W. I. (1966), *On Social Organization and Personality*, University of Chicago Press.

THRASHER, F. M. (1927), *The Gang*. Reprinted by University of Chicago Press (1963).

TOBIAS, J. J. (1967), *Crime and Industrial Society in the Nineteenth Century*, London: Batsford.

VOLD, G. B. (1958), *Theoretical Criminology*, New York: Oxford University Press.

WALKER, N. (1965), *Crime and Punishment in Great Britain*, Edinburgh University Press.

WALKER, N. (1967), 'A Century of Causal Theory', in H. Klare and D. Haxby, eds., *Frontiers in Criminology*, London: Pergamon Press.

WALLERSTEIN, J. S. and WYLE, C. (1947), 'Our Law-Abiding Law Breakers', *Probation*, Vol. 25, pp. 107-12.

BIBLIOGRAPHY

WEBER, M. (1949), *The Methodology of the Social Sciences*, Chicago: Free Press.

WHYTE, W. F. (1943), *Street Corner Society*. Reprinted by University of Chicago Press (1966).

WILES, P. and CARSON, W. G., eds. (1971), *Crime and Delinquency in Britain: sociological readings*, London: Martin Robertson.

WILKINS, L. (1964), *Social Policy, Action and Research*, London: Tavistock Publications.

WILKINS, L. (1965), 'Evaluation of Penal Treatments' in P. Halmos, ed. (1965).

WILSON, H. (1962), *Delinquency and Child Neglect*, London: Allen & Unwin.

WINTER, G. (1966), *Elements for a Social Ethic*, New York: Macmillan.

WIRTH, L. (1964), *On Cities and Social Life*, University of Chicago Press.

WOLFGANG, M., SAVITZ, L. and JOHNSTON, N., eds. (1962), *The Sociology of Crime and Delinquency*, New York: John Wiley.

WOLFGANG, M. and FERRACUTI, F. (1967) *The Sub-culture of Violence*, London: Tavistock Publications.

WOOTTON, B. (1963), *Crime and the Criminal Law*, London: Stevens.

YABLONSKY, L. (1967), *The Violent Gang*, London: Penguin Books.